Upon Whom We Depend

Studies in the
Postmodern Theory of Education

Joe L. Kincheloe and Shirley R. Steinberg
General Editors

Vol. 98

PETER LANG
New York • Washington, D.C./Baltimore • Boston
Bern • Frankfurt am Main • Berlin • Vienna • Paris

J. Gordon Chamberlin

Upon Whom We Depend

The American Poverty System

PETER LANG
New York • Washington, D.C./Baltimore • Boston
Bern • Frankfurt am Main • Berlin • Vienna • Paris

Library of Congress Cataloging-in-Publication Data

Chamberlin, J. Gordon (John Gordon).
Upon whom we depend: the American poverty system / J. Gordon Chamberlin.
p. cm. — (Counterpoints; vol. 98)
Includes bibliographical references and index.
1. Poverty—United States. 2. Poor—United States. 3. Social classes—United
States. I. Title. II. Series: Counterpoints (New York, N.Y.); vol. 98.
HC110.P6C326   339.4'6'0973—dc21   98-26799
ISBN 0-8204-4151-1
ISSN 1058-1634

Die Deutsche Bibliothek-CIP-Einheitsaufnahme

Chamberlin, J. Gordon:
Upon whom we depend: the American poverty system / J. Gordon Chamberlin.
–New York; Washington, D.C./Baltimore; Boston; Bern;
Frankfurt am Main; Berlin; Vienna; Paris: Lang.
(Counterpoints; Vol. 98)
ISBN 0-8204-4151-1

Cover design by Andy Ruggirello

The paper in this book meets the guidelines for permanence and durability
of the Committee on Production Guidelines for Book Longevity
of the Council of Library Resources.

© 1999 Peter Lang Publishing, Inc., New York

Printed in the United States of America

CONTENTS

we always

begin

in the middle

Chapter 1

ALL OF US

All of us come into the world the same way. Each of us arrives with distinct characteristics shaped by the joined genetic streams of our parents. For all of us, that arrival is a social encounter, for we then join a long and wide stream of human activity. It is a powerful stream from which we cannot escape, because all of us are social creatures.

Each of us arrives in a particular locale where we encounter, very early, an elaborate arrangement of social patterns, practices, and structures. For most of us our first encounter with the structures of society is in the hospital where doctors and nurses, and all of the paraphernalia of modern medical science, are employed to deliver us from the constricted environment of the womb.

Unknowingly, of course, we also encounter the world of ideas when the obstetrician decides whether to do this or that procedure. We feel the differences of our relationship to nurses, who have ideas about what is to be done with us, and our mothers who have different ideas of who we are and what to do with us. Then we hear "girl" or "boy" and all the sounds of endless talk about babies introduce us to the distinctly human capacity of speech. When we leave the hospital to enter our home we encounter more social structures and patterns as we begin the lifelong process of being a family member. Each step of expanded context involves us in the very human tension between individual desires and the claims of society. No matter what direction we look we see that we are related to others, whether it is to people just across the street or to the whole human family that occupies our global island floating in space. No matter what we discuss or learn about, from microbes to glaciers, we soon discover that in each subject we are all bound together. Everything happening in the world eventually affects us all.

The fact that we are bound together in so many ways does not mean that we are united as a happy family. We are divided by many kinds of beliefs, desires, loyalties, and passions. These give meaning and connectedness to members of large and small groups, clubs, and nations, parties and religions, but they can also divide us into contentious and warring factions.

Across the lines of party, nation, and religion within that global family there is another kind of divide which prompts the concerns we address here, the divide in every society between those who are poor and those who are not.

Considering poverty involves repeated emphasis on the relationship of the individual to the larger social setting and to the roles of different social structures.

Understanding poverty requires that we recognize how it functions as an essential feature of the social structure which we all share.

I offer the ideas and views spelled out in the following chapters, assuming that you also have ideas and views about the subject, perhaps well established. They may include strongly held feelings and beliefs which are difficult to set aside in order to consider the validity of other views.

Our exploration assumes that most people who study poverty and attempt to help the poor do so from the perspective of their own experiences and concerns. Scholarship has produced a rich literature about the poor. The concern and generosity of millions of caregivers have led to establishing thousands of agencies, both public and private, to help the poor. The focus of both scholarship and programs on the consequences of poverty has nurtured the widespread assumption that the causes of poverty are the handicaps, deprivation, and failures of the poor themselves. Our many service programs, therefore, are designed to meet the needs of poor individuals and families and are motivated by the awareness that poverty's threat to our nation's fabric is a threat to all of us.

Deep concern about the consequences of poverty has raised millions of dollars in charity and prompted the spending of billions more on government programs to feed the hungry, shelter the homeless, and heal the sick. Some poor people have benefitted from these efforts. Spending has focused on the handicapped, the troubled, the jobless, and those caught in a web of inadequacies. Despite all of this, poverty continues.

One reason for the failure of those efforts to overcome poverty is their neglect of a far larger portion of the poor, those on whom we depend for the multitude of essential services which benefit us, the nonpoor. Equal attention, study, and care have not been given to the structures and practices of the society we share which perpetuate poverty. Dealing with the threat of poverty requires, first, that we understand the poverty system.

The objective of this book is to explore ways to expand our comprehension, to bring a more holistic and balanced perspective which leads to action on this vast social blight.

Understanding is not a finicky word. It can be used as a noun or a verb or an adjective. Even as a noun it can refer to two modes of thought. For some, to understand is to arrive at the *right* way to think about a matter: "You should understand that . . ." For others, the term refers to a step in a longer process that, in a sense, never "arrives" but indicates where one is in the ongoing effort to learn an appropriate way to think of where we are. It is to say, "as I now understand the matter." This way of thinking implies a kind of dialogue between what is happening and how we interpret it. John Dewey explained that "experience" is not the happening but the interpreting. He contended that we do this all of the time. Every event in our lives, from the trivial to the ponderous, prompts some kind of interpretation.

Thus, "understanding" comes from thinking about a matter, which means that understanding is always a posteriori. We cannot understand something that has not yet happened. Nor can we understand something we have not encountered. We can grasp the needs of a homeless family and with a thoroughly human response attempt to help them find a home. But it is much more difficult to comprehend the full consequences of the event and the enormous social reality of worldwide poverty. Of course, those who accept the common canard that being poor is one's own fault would not be able to consider such a connection.

Recognizing that poverty can be a distinct field of study inevitably leads to realizing its multiple dimensions and that understanding poverty involves the same kind of effort as it takes to understand any mammoth physical object, like a mountain.

One step in understanding the complexity of that object comes when we view the mountain from all four directions, or even from above. It looks different from each perspective but we know the varied views are of the same object. We can easily recognize that biology, botany, physics, geology, and hydrology are all necessary and all interrelated in order to understand the mountain's physical characteristics.

In the same way various disciplines such as economics, sociology, psychology, physiology, political science, literature, history, and ethics are needed to understand the interrelated dimension and scope of poverty.

The analogy can be expanded by seeing effects humans have had on the mountain by the roads, buildings, dams, mines, as well as effects the mountain has had on people who may have spent their honeymoon on the south side, had a favorite ski slope on the north side, or been devastated by a volcanic eruption. Both direct experience and reading about the experience of others share in shaping what the mountain means to us. We realize that every mountain has a history, and an adequate understanding of its role, power, and effects on humans and other creatures depends on studying that history, whether it be that of Vesuvius, Kilimanjaro or Mount St. Helens. And our individual encounters with mountains are built into our memories.

It is surely obvious that in order to understand poverty we need to study its terrible history from the untouchables of India, to the slave trade in nearly every country (including our own), and to the feudal and the industrial pattern of treatment for those at the bottom. All of this history resides in our social genes and is incorporated into our collective memories.

An adequate understanding of poverty needs to be equally inclusive because we will be involved with it either directly or indirectly for the rest of our lives. Just as the understanding of any other subject or object changes as new realities are brought into our consciousness, so too our views of poverty will change as we reinterpret experience and information in terms of our own situation, present and future.

In other words, understanding comes from reflection. Actually most of us reflect again and again on the important matters of our lives, and our interpretation may change as we grow older, or in other contexts, or when we are involved with others as we remember or explain. This aspect of living is a continuing dialogue between participation and reflection. Poverty is a vast field with many historical and contemporary dimensions but, unfortunately, it is seldom studied in a systematic way.

One reason seems to be that when concerned and benevolent people see or hear what poverty does to other families, children, and old people, they are moved to do something about it promptly. What causes and perpetuates poverty seems so obvious to them that studying it could appear to be a form of excuse or escape.

The way we interpret the problems of poverty will inevitably affect our decisions about action. We assume that ideas presented here may be quite different from commonly held perspectives about what is happening to the poor in this society. And, should the assumption be correct, time is needed for the inner dialogue a reader may have between one's present views and those presented here.

Some chapters are followed by a variety of items that may stimulate further thinking about what is presented in the body of the chapter. This suggests a hope that, for most, this does not become a "one sitting" read. I hope that you will read a chapter and let it percolate for a while before returning to read the next chapter. Each chapter offers both the presentation of a significant issue, and additional material for further reflection on it.

In the early 1980s five members of a committee assigned to do something about the poor in their county thought it would be well to start by listing the reasons, other than race and gender, why people are in poverty. Thinking their list might encourage discussion, they decided to put it in a booklet, adding comments from staff members of related agencies, and having a local artist provide illustrations. Here is a copy of the result.[1]

6

ADDICTION

"The chemically dependent person is at risk for health, legal problems, and job loss. The drug can dictate life, become a daily preoccupation, destroy relationships of trust, strain familial ties, and disintegrate self-respect. Addiction is a poverty of mind and soul as well as of body and finances."
KATHY S. JORDAN, DRUG ACTION COUNCIL

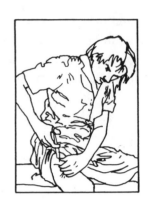

CATASTROPHIC ILLNESS

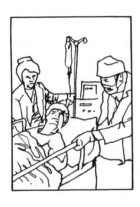

"The costs of medical care for a catastrophic illness such as leukemia or cancer are usually astronomical. Unfortunately, such illnesses are common in low income families, are diagnosed later, and often treated less adequately. All of these things tend to cause or perpetuate poverty."
DONALD M. HAYES, MD, AMERICAN CANCER SOCIETY

CYCLE OF POVERTY

"The phrase cycle of poverty conveys the idea that, generation after generation, poverty is transmitted from poor parents to their children. Studies show that this is most likely in work: those of low occupational positions tend to have parents similarly placed: 7% of AFDC caseloads are multigenerational."
ANDREW N. DOBELSTEIN, PROFESSOR OF SOCIAL WORK

DISABLED

"Although disabled persons work in a variety of jobs, poverty can strike when a person is either unable to work or unable to find a job because employers are unwilling to hire someone with a known disability. If not found eligible for Social Service benefits, the person has no source of income."

ALICE S. DAVIS, VOCATIONAL REHABILITATION SERVICES

DISASTER

"In the heated debate over who is poor and why, one reason rarely gets discussed: poverty because of disaster. There are natural disasters like floods and tornadoes; economic disasters now devastating farms; and personal disasterlike auto accidents, being a victim of crime, or in the family of a criminal."

ROBERT J. WINEBURG, PROFESSOR OF SOCIAL WORK

DROPPED OUT OF LABOR MARKET

"Because our society tends to favor younger persons, the chances of unemployed persons over forty being hired to the same or comparable positions become extremely difficult. After trying long and hard without success they drop out and try no more. And inexperienced youth add to the thousands of the discouraged."

VINCENT U. COLUMNA, EQUAL EMPLOYMENT OPPORTUNITY COMMISSION

ELDERLY WITH ONLY SOCIAL SECURITY

"For about 60% of men, 65 or older, in the population, Social Security is the primary source of income. For 60% of women, 65 or older, Social Security is the sole or exclusive source of income. Even with Social Security, women receive far less proportionately."
JAMES C. CARPENTER, UNITED SERVICES FOR OLDER ADULTS

ELDERLY WITHOUT SOCIAL SECURITY

"Without Social Security the statistics are especially serious for single elderly women. If one is old and Black and a woman, the prospects are alarming. Many of them live in deplorable circumstances with meager access to food. Many are homebound, a problem in both urban and rural areas."
JAMES C. CARPENTER, UNITED SERVICES FOR OLDER ADULTS

EMPLOYED AT MINIMUM WAGE

"Many businesses thrive by paying minimum wage or slightly above, making it difficult for a person to advance in the company. To advance often requires mobility which many workers do not have. It is a vicious circle. By working employees part time, companies cut costs and often pay few or no fringe benefits."
THOMAS B. REYNOLDS, III, EMPLOYMENT SECURITY COMMISSION

IN PRISON

"Most people in prison are poor, and prison keeps them poor. It doesn't prepare them for meaningful employment when they get out. We say they have paid their debt to society, but it is very difficult to get folks jobs when they have been in the system. This society is sometimes very punitive."
YVONNE J. JOHNSON, SENTENCING ALTERNATIVE CENTER

MENTAL ILLNESS

"Mental illness is like other illnesses. It can be temporary, but not everyone recovers. Prejudice and misunderstanding can impede employment opportunities. Poverty can result from stigma, low morale, loss of self-esteem, medication side effects, poor work record and unrealistic expectations."
BEVERLY I. WILLIAMS, MENTAL HEALTH ASSOCIATION

MENTAL RETARDATION

"A majority of people with mental retardation can learn skills that make them good employees. They take pride in their work. By the nature of their handicaps, they are limited to jobs at low wages. Mentally retarded adults often depend upon the human services delivery system to meet their needs."
BECKY WOOD, ASSOCIATION FOR RETARDED CITIZENS

MIGRANT WORKERS

"Migrant workers stoop all day in the hot sun picking cucumbers and scraping sweet potatoes out of the earth with bare hands. They give us food and are key to the survival of agriculture in many states. But we keep them invisible, not providing decent wages or living conditions."
EVELYN MATTERN, STATE COUNCIL OF
CHURCHES

PHYSICALLY HANDICAPPED

"There aren't many employers who would acquire special equipment in order to offer employment to blind persons. There is a social hesitation to employ a deformed person, particularly for a job requiring public contacts. If two equally competent persons apply for a job, the less handicapped person is likely to get it."
RICHARD J. GORHAM, GOODWILL INDUSTRIES

REFUGEES

"Refugees are people forced to flee their homeland because of well founded fear of persecution based on race, religion or political beliefs. Most are fleeing war. On arrival they are indigent. Most become self-sufficient, but many remain near poverty for lack of training in the English language, Western jobs, etc."
RALEIGH BAILEY, REFUGEE RESETTLEMENT
PROGRAM

TEEN SINGLE PARENT

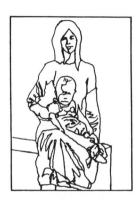

"Single teenage mothers face almost certain poverty with no breadwinning father present. Teen mothers: fail to complete education, fail to get good paying jobs, often enter health care system late in pregnancy, frequently repeat pregnancies, are less likely to marry, if married their divorce rate is higher, and have more child abuse."

EMILY T. TYLER, PUBLIC HEALTH DEPARTMENT

UNDER EDUCATED

"Not possessing basic math and English skills required by employers, not being able to fill out an application properly or understand a written instruction, to work at a dead end job with little or no chance of advancement---that is what it means to be under educated. This is what we hear from our students."

DORINDA L. GILLIAM, COMMUNITY COLLEGE

UNEMPLOYED

"In smaller towns when a company has to close, often there are not other plants to hire all those put out of work. People who have worked 20-30 years for the company find it difficult to go into a different field. While retraining and looking for other work, unemployment benefits up to 26 weeks average $115.21 a week."

THOMAS B. REYNOLDS, III, EMPLOYMENT SECURITY COMMISSION

BAD LUCK

"Says one authority, in large organizations the greatest factor in success is sheer, unadulterated luck. For persons of equal endowment and energy, many factors can make the difference between those who make it and others who may end up in poverty. There are some in poverty for no other reason."

J. DON REEVES, PROFESSOR OF EDUCATION

Chapter 2

WHERE WE ARE

We already know about poverty. We know facts and statistics; we know the kinds of people who are poor; we have our own ideas of why they are in that condition; and we have our own views about the way they behave and think. We know that poverty is a worldwide problem, and that in this country many kinds of government and private agencies have been set up to help the needy with food, housing, clothing, etc. In fact, some of us are directly involved in conducting such agencies.

Furthermore, we realize that for most of us this is not an easy matter to discuss. It is not something we banter about at lunch with fellow employees or when we have friends over for a picnic. We seldom hear about it if we go to church. The study of poverty is not part of the curriculum in most universities. As a matter of fact, poverty is a subject we would rather not have to think about.

Yet we recognize that someone has to think about it because it is a frightful blight all over the world. Although this country moves along in a $7 trillion economy with a per capita income of over $30,000 a year, millions of our fellow citizens go hungry, have no place to live, have no doctor even if they are working full-time. The numerous welfare programs of federal and state governments and even more numerous non-governmental charitable activities have not been able to slow the advance of poverty.

Doing something realistic about the puzzle of poverty requires an understanding of how and why its grip on our society is so tenacious. Helping readers gain some of that understanding is our objective. This requires that we start with where we are, recognizing that no two of us have had the same experiences with poverty, nor that we interpret our experiences in the same way.

Undoubtedly for you and others, the matters discussed in this chapter will be something of a review rather than an introduction to new ideas or data. But as you proceed you will recognize that the approach to the subject in what follows has grown from a commitment to an inclusive, holistic view, because we believe that understanding comes from seeing how the different aspects of poverty are related to each other. The question is, what kind of approach can make sense of that interrelationship?

Our approach will engage us first in reexamining what we already know. Obviously, how we interpret what we know depends upon our family background, where we have lived, the level of our family income, our social experiences, the views of influential friends, what our teachers have had to say about it, the common assumptions of people in our community, and the television programs we watch or the newspapers we read.

To assist in such a review the following "Examining One's Own Exposure to Poverty" outline may be useful. It is not intended as an exercise, but as a suggestion of things to reflect on to see how our present views of poverty have been shaped.

Examining One's Own Exposure to Poverty

My encounters with the poor have been: first as a child, youth, adult; initiated by me, initiated by a poor person, in a group, for a short time or an extended period; in school, at work, in church, in community meetings, at music concerts, in staff meetings, at play.

When I think "poor" I usually think: male, female, white, black, Hispanic, Asian, old, young.

My conversations with the poor have been about: family, school, work, jobs, the weather, entertainment, athletics, a meal being served, convictions, income, friends, teachers, the news.

When I think about the poor I picture their: personal views, income, behavior, intelligence, homes, communities, problems.

My sources of information about the poor have been and are: my parents, friends, teachers, preachers, the poor themselves, fellow employees, books, magazines, movies, radio, television, newspapers.

My impression of the general attitude toward the poor held by the public at large is: admiration, hostility, fear, disapproval of their behavior, respect, disgust, sympathy, wanting to help them, shaped by stereotypes, based on limited exposure, or other feelings.

Another step is to reflect on what we think about what we know. Each of us has feelings, beliefs, ethical judgments, and assumptions about human nature, as well as concepts of political rights and responsibilities. We may have some feelings of guilt because we have not done what we could, or we may feel a bit of pride because we are charitable and we sympathize with the unfortunate, or we may be disgusted about the way the poor behave or about how they are treated in this society. Only when we are frank with ourselves about why we assume, know, and think as we do, are we ready to move on to consider other perspectives about the domain called "poverty."

The third step will be to consider, with equal care and responsibility, the fundamental causes of poverty and its perpetuation. But before we dig deeper it is necessary to clarify what we mean by the terms we are using.

Terminology

We begin by looking at two terms. Each has problems.

In common usage, the terms "poor" and "poverty" are assumed to be synonymous. In announcing a study by the National Center for Children in Poverty at Columbia University's School of Public Health, a fact sheet points out that from 1987 to 1992 the number of *poor* children under age six in the United States rose from five to six million.

Poverty rates for children under age six were highest in urban areas. Most government reports make the same assumption about the use of the two words.

Some of us, however, distinguish between the two words when we say, "That family is poor but they are not in poverty," or "We were poor but we were never in poverty," implying that poverty is a deeper level of poorness. In other words "poor" can be used as a more inclusive concept, but "in poverty" suggests a distinction.

It will help our consideration of this very large field if we look at the more inclusive term "poor" first. But thinking about the situation of the poor poses an annoying problem because it is always relative. "Poor" means different things to different people.

Poor refers to economics, doesn't it? Well, not always. It is a tramp adjective that accompanies many kinds of nouns. There is "I'm a poor bridge player" or "That is very poor soil" or "Fred has been doing poorly lately" or "Victor is a poor loser" or "Our pastor is a nice person but that was a poor sermon," etc. The word has many different uses.

Even when limiting it to an economic context it can still have a wide range of connotations. Test it for yourself. In a group, have each person fill out and hand back an unsigned card with these two items on it:

Number of persons in my family ____

Annual income needed to not be poor $ _____

Then see the differences.

That exercise indicates the subjective meaning of the term and shows how widely views of "poor" vary. However, when the term is moved into a social context it indicates an assumption that there is a common objective basis for determining what "poor" means. When someone asks about the number of poor in a school, a city, or the nation, we get our answer from the Census Bureau which uses a "line" established by the federal government to identify who is "in poverty." Thus in common usage "poor" has come to mean "below the poverty line."

This significant gap, between what poor means to us personally and what it means officially for the government, causes confusion both in the relative nature of the term "poor," and in differences among us about the level of income that has been adopted in the use of the term, "poverty line."

The Poverty Line

The poverty line, developed in the 1950s, reflected studies which indicated that the cost of food was about one-third of a family's total cost of living.

The Department of Agriculture assigned the task of determining minimal adequate nutritional needs of families to its Consumer Nutrition

Division. Food costs were then estimated on three levels of nutritional intake. Since the purpose of having a "line" is to determine who is "poor," and therefore entitled to assistance, the lowest level is called "The Thrifty Food Plan."

Changes have been made from time to time in the nutritional standards for a minimal food plan, and in recent years the total costs have been adjusted in keeping with the general cost of living. According to the Division the nutritional decisions of 1983 are still valid. See the next page.

A national "poverty line" provides a baseline for statisticians and for general planning but it has not eliminated confusion in determining who is entitled to federal welfare programs. In fact, several years ago Congress asked the National Academy of Sciences to consider the many problems which have arisen in trying to have a standard for "means" tested programs that could apply equally across the country. The Academy reported that trying to establish a standard amount for the nation posed too many problems. Since the 1960s the many changes in styles of living, costs of housing, differences between regions as well as between rural and urban settings, have made a single national "line" increasingly irrelevant and unfair.

It is important to remember, as we look at the problems of poverty, that it is those who are not poor who are often confused, who believe it is possible to have a "means" test for welfare programs and who have designed that test. Most of us do not know that living in "poor" areas means that the cost of food is higher for them than it is for us. Thus we are never exposed to the consequences for the poor of a common national "poverty line" upon which welfare programs are based.

Although the words poverty and poor may be seen as synonymous (even by Webster), in common discourse they are often used differently in at least two ways. Poverty, for many, refers to being destitute or indigent. In that usage there would be a sharp difference between the "poor line" and the "poverty line," particularly if poor is based on our subjective views. "Poor" could have many levels, with poverty as the lowest. In other words, there can be many poor families whose annual incomes are above the "poverty line."

Look at this carefully. If you have a teenage son would you expect him to be content with 2/10 of a cup of soft drink a day?

This page is taken from a publication, THE THRIFTY FOOD PLAN, 1983, of the Consumer Nutrition Division, U.S. Department of Agriculture, Hyattsville, Maryland 20782, August 1983. It describes daily food requirements and costs that, multiplied by three, determine the "poverty threshold" for various family sizes. The weekly costs listed here are as of June, 1982. They have been increased since in keeping with changes in the general price index.

This food plan is used as the basis for the coupon allotment for the Food Stamp Program. Its revision in 1983 was to take into account new information about nutritional needs, nutritional values of foods, food consumption, and food prices.

Table 2.1 Thrifty Food Plan, 1983: A Day's Food as Served

Food¹	Unit	Child (years)				Male (years)				Female (years)		
		1-2	3-5	6-8	9-11	12-14	15-19	20-50	51 and over	12-19	20-50	51 and over
Weekly cost as of June, 1982		$9.30	10.00	12.20	14.50	15.30	15.90	16.90	15.50	15.30	15.40	15.30
		Number of units per day										
Vegetables, fruit	½ c.	2.1	2.5	3.4	4.0	3.7	3.8	4.3	3.9	3.9	4.9	4.6
Cereal, pasta, dry	1 oz.²	2.6	2.6	2.7	2.9	3.2	3.3	2.7	2.6	2.9	2.6	2.4
Bread³	1 slice	3.0	4.3	6.2	6.7	8.6	8.3	8.4	7.4	5.6	5.8	4.2
Bakery products¹	1 slice	.1	.2	.9	1.2	.4	.9	1.2	.7	.8	.3	.2
Milk, yogurt	1 c.	1.8	1.5	1.7	2.1	1.9	1.9	.9	.7	2.2	1.1	1.0
Cheese (per week)	1 oz.	.6	.8	1.2	1.6	1.6	1.6	2.0	1.9	4.1	4.4	4.8
Meat, poultry, fish, boned⁴	1 oz.	2.0	2.0	2.1	2.4	3.0	3.5	4.0	4.3	3.1	4.1	4.5
Eggs (per week)	no.	2.8	2.7	1.8	2.4	2.1	3.0	3.9	4.1	3.9	4.2	3.9
Dry beans, peas, cooked; nuts	½ c.	.4	.4	.3	.4	1.0	.9	.7	1.0	.5	.7	.6
Fats, oils	1 tbsp.	.5	1.2	2.3	2.7	2.9	3.7	3.1	2.3	.7	.9	.7
Sugar, sweets	1 tbsp.	.3	1.6	3.7	4.2	5.9	4.3	4.9	3.6	1.2	.7	.8
Soft drinks, punches, ades	1 c.	.1	.1	.2	.2	.2	.4	.3	.1	.3	.1	.1

¹Excludes commercially prepared mixtures except bread and bakery products.

²1 oz. of dry cereal or pasta is about 1 serving.

³Bread is commercially prepared bread and bread assumed to be made at home from flour and meal and some milk, fat, and sugar, in terms of food as purchased. Ingredients used other than flour and meal in homemade bakery products in excess of those required to make bread are included in the group of the ingredient. Bakery products shown are only commercially prepared types.

⁴Lean parts of meat and poultry. Includes some bacon, sausage, and luncheon meats.

An additional confusion is introduced when poverty in the United States is compared with poverty in other countries. It is often pointed out how much better off our poor are than those in Bangladesh, Burundi, or Haiti. The matter of context in relation to poverty deserves attention later. We have not yet examined some of the other words which contribute to the confusion.

One of those words is "welfare." Among the many programs introduced in the 1930s was Aid to Families with Dependent Children, AFDC. It was intended primarily for widows with children. It was called "welfare," and over the years many professionals have meant that particular program when they say "welfare." Now, however, in common usage the word welfare blankets a multitude of programs for the poor, for the rich, for farmers, for industries, etc. And this has led to much concern as we contrast government benefits for the poor with benefits for those of us who are not poor.

Welfare programs have become known as "entitlements," implying that once enacted they are impossible to withdraw. But that connotation is now under a severe test, particularly in programs of welfare for the poor who lack political clout to protect their interests. One result is that the "conversation" going on in the country at this time is not about poverty, but about "welfare," who should conduct it, and who should pay for it. This quick turning of attention to "what to do" without a diagnosis of basic causes is very American. We are doers, and often seem to believe that all social problems are solvable.

This may be so, but what do we mean by "solving"? For some it means getting poverty off our radar screen. Too often in the past we have "solved" social problems by moving them elsewhere and leaving them for others to handle. These are false prescriptions because they are based on inadequate knowledge. An adequate diagnosis must address both basic causes of poverty and the many institutional and cultural structures of our society which share in perpetuating poverty.

Chapter 3

OUR SOCIAL ARRANGEMENT

When we think of poverty we think of poor people, that is, people lacking resources. For the last fifty years and more, concern for the poor has focused almost exclusively upon persons, on their problems and behavior, as well as their needs for food, housing, and job training. That concern has produced thousands of studies, mountains of statistics, and numberless stories and books, written by the nonpoor as they analyzed the situations of the poor. Those books, commission reports, foundation funded studies, and volumes of regulations now crowd the shelves of college and university libraries.

The concentrated focus on the poor over many decades has been based on the assumption that overcoming poverty required the thousands of programs conducted by millions of devoted people and costing billions of dollars. Many different kinds of organizations have shared in the effort to help the poor survive and, hopefully, work their way up the ladder so they will no longer need our assistance.

This tremendous enterprise has been supported by the public at large and its basic assumptions have been taken for granted. Now it is obvious that the programs have not overcome poverty and that those assumptions were inadequate. The enterprise failed because those who studied the problems and designed the policies, both public and private, failed to recognize the word's other connotation. Poverty also refers to a social arrangement by which the poor, while providing for essential needs of the non-poor, receive wages that are less than it costs them to live. This is systemic poverty and it is the domain of the employed poor.

Considering the persistence of poverty involves examining both personal *and* social causes, and that may be difficult for most of us.

The views we now hold, shaped by that limited approach and its commonly accepted assumptions, will probably make it difficult for us now to consider a very different way to address the blight of poverty.

We have shared with others in supporting United Way, we have contributed to charity in our churches and synagogues, we have tried not to accept stereotypes about how poor people act, and we have definite opinions about federal welfare. We have thought we were doing the right thing and fulfilling our social responsibilities. Right! It is difficult to face criticism of what we have assumed.

What we are now doing is not wrong, it is just on one track when it should be on two. It is obvious that government and private programs are necessary. They have provided and continue to provide housing for the homeless, food for the hungry, and healing to the ill. We know that many people criticize those programs because they are convinced that the poor bring their poverty on themselves. We know that other people have grown tired after pouring time, money, and energy into those programs. The idea of studying poverty in the hope of finding a better way does not appeal to either mindset. Nor is such study very attractive to those presently committed to programs of help because they are convinced that what is now being done is the best that can be done under the circumstances. They are comfortable with the common assumptions about the poor.

However, if we are still concerned about what it is doing to our society, the study of poverty should open doors to the examination of more fundamental reasons for its persistence. And that examination needs to begin by clarifying our "social arrangement."

Unfortunately many of those who analyze society's failure to overcome poverty start with an ethical critique of indifference, insensitivity, and irresponsibility. They attack exploitation and greed, and urge society to recognize how unfairly we treat the poor.

There is a place for such moral outrage, but that should follow, not precede, a careful analysis of causes. If an individual, an institution, or a country is committed to correcting either a personal or a social problem, the first requirement is an accurate description of what already is, rather than starting with what should be. Commitment to overcoming the blight of poverty requires recognizing that changes must be made, but first there must be an openness to dimensions that are quite new for us. Here we attempt to describe as objectively as possible the arrangement by which poverty fulfills a distinctive role in our social structure. We will consider prescriptions later.

Every society, past and present, has developed a way for getting "bottom jobs" done. Greeks and Romans enslaved prisoners of war who fed the hogs, dug the vegetables, built temples, cooked meals, cleaned houses, and took care of children. Some slaves were freed but the system continued because others took their places.

In medieval feudalism the manor system often was based on an exchange by which vassals could keep some of what they raised on their land as long as they were available to fight the wars of the lord of the manor. In both systems the slave owner or lord was responsible for the food, clothing, housing, health, and spiritual welfare of slaves or serfs.

The industrial revolution introduced a different pattern in which workers doing bottom jobs would receive wages but would have to turn to others for help in meeting the rest of their needs.

In her book *The Dispossessed*, historian Jacqueline Jones describes in considerable detail many variations of ways by which employers limited their responsibilities to employees. After the Civil War, plantation owners in this country needed the former slaves on their plantations for only part of the year when cotton, rice, and sugar were planted and harvested, so to keep black labor for the full year they developed "annual contracts," which promised payments on December 31. During the slack season, survival depended on charity.[2]

In many ways the poverty system has been modified over the last three hundred years. Still it provides the general pattern for America's present social arrangement by which employers provide part of what it costs their employees to live while the society at large provides the rest. On the surface this would appear as a form of subsidy for poor workers. But it can also be recognized as subsidizing their employers. In fact it is a "survival arrangement," for unless workers survive, there would be no one to perform the essential low-status jobs which enable employers to enjoy their profits, and all of us to enjoy numerous conveniences and benefits, as well as lower prices. However, this arrangement has very high social costs.

From Employment	From Charity
	Food
	Clothing
Wages	Housing
	Medical services
	Child care
	Transportation

= Survival

These high social costs derive from the consequences of poor education, poor housing, lack of preventive medical care, and lack of opportunities. Our society pays those costs many times over through other very expensive channels. Meanwhile the arrangement is both inefficient and demeaning.

In our daily activities we seldom think about this set-up. We take for granted our subsidized benefits and conveniences; our costs that are low because of low wages paid to people who check us out at the grocery store, who wait on our table at the restaurant, who harvest the fruits and vegetables for that meal, or who bus our children to school. The list is very long. These people, and millions more like them, constitute a major sector in our society.

The familiar term "sector" is most frequently used to distinguish between the "public" and "private" realms. But the private sector can be divided into many sub-sectors: farming, manufacturing, entertainment, professions, services, and other kinds of activities.

Most studies of the structure of our social system have focused on "class," and arguments over the meaning of that term have gone on ever since Karl Marx identified class with ownership and Max Weber identified it with status.

Preoccupation with class on the part of sociologists and economists has caused them to miss the crucial distinction with which we are now concerned: the distinction within the "lower" class between the poor who are employed and the poor who are not employed.

Analyzing the problems of poverty in terms of "work," shifts our focus from the behavior of individuals to the functions of institutions.

Essential Sectors

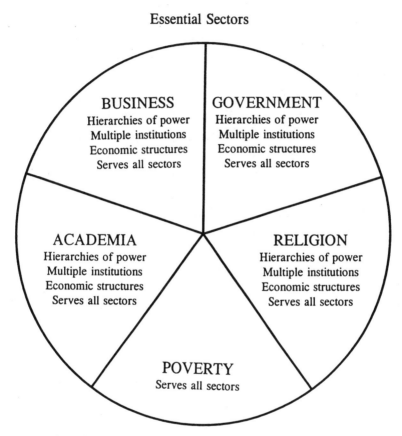

Those functions are essential to the survival of every class in society. Each sector is significant because of its distinctive institutional functions. Each type of institution has hierarchies of leadership with responsibility to administer particular patterns and practices in order to carry on the sector's work.

Institutions are the primary means by which all of us find our place in the world, a sense of belonging, sustenance, and employment. They

26

are the mechanism for working together. They provide stability. They are shaped by our history. Ingrained in their structures and practices are our commonly held cultural, social, religious, and economic values. And in them our assumptions about social responsibility have been institutionalized. Each of us can easily make a menu of institutions with which we identify ourselves, and by which we are identified. Those institutions sustain the general welfare because they are also units of social power by which the non-poor guide and control social developments and changes. In them the assumptions which undergird the way we address poverty are reinforced.

Each sector serves all others. To the major sectors of academia, business, government, and religion must be added a fifth, the poverty sector which also serves all others. The poverty sector is like the others. Its responsibilities constitute a distinctive role, but it is significantly different because it has no institutions and no hierarchy of leadership. Occasionally the labor movement has attempted to provide leadership in this sector but only on a limited basis. The poverty sector is not a unit of social power, so does not have power to solve the social problem it poses.

The simplistic idea that poverty can be overcome by education of the poor, or by more effort and self-reliance on their part, so that then they will be able to climb the ladder into the middle class, fails to recognize the necessity of those low-status jobs. Someone has to do them, regardless of how many individuals climb out. Our help to individuals does not, and cannot, address the system.

This means that the fate of those who make up the poverty sector, who do the many kinds of low-status work that are essential to the welfare of everyone, is in the hands of those with power, the rest of us. And it has always been so, whether in Greece and Rome, medieval England, or in the slaveholding South or the industrial North of the United States.

Those concerned about poverty usually focus statistics to indicate the extent of particular needs in order to determine programs and costs. But diagnosing causes of poverty, both of origin and of perpetuation, cannot be resolved so mathematically. However, since we are so accustomed to beginning the study of a problem by checking the numbers, it may be important to have a current reality check to assure ourselves that what we are considering is a very serious social problem.

According to a 1994 Census Bureau report on *Income, Poverty and Valuation* (Series P60-189), 89,798,000 persons live in households with annual incomes less than twice the poverty line. One third of the children in this country under 18 years of age, 30,772,000 of them, live in those households. They are poor.

Reasons for the perpetuation of poverty are a tangle of roots which cannot be separated, and many go very deep. It is an economic matter, but economic values stem from other more basic values; *responsibility*, both individual and social, which can lead to conflict; *freedom* that must be curbed for some so that it is available to all; *justice* that requires limitations of power; and *work* which is both a necessity and a virtue that is relative to the status accorded to different kinds of jobs.

It is these cultural values, beliefs, and commitments which make it possible for most of us to take for granted the present arrangement. So, examining the attitudes, points of view, and basic values of the public at large provides a clue as to why poverty persists. This needs to be part of the diagnosis.

It comes close to home for all of us. We would have great difficulty doing what our ancestors did, with all of these jobs done at home by family members. We are a specialized society and need the poverty sector to provide the following services:

      cleaning our homes
      taking care of our children
      busing our students to school
      assisting our teachers
      tending to our grandparents
      aiding our nurses
      assembling our appliances
      processing meat, fish, and poultry
      harvesting our vegetables
      checking out our groceries
      serving us fast food

        janitoring in our churches
        housekeeping our motel rooms
        checking us into hotels
        washing our dishes
        sewing our clothes
        cleaning and pressing our suits and shirts
        clerking for our retail purchases, and
        cleaning our toilets.
In consequence, they
        live in poor housing in danger of crime
        are often hungry
        have more medical problems
        cannot afford health insurance
        have more legal problems
        can never save for emergencies
        cannot provide for their own pensions,
While we,
        have help on which we depend
        are freed from essential tasks
        get food at lower costs
        pay less for personal services
        get better medical care
        live in greater safety
        can prepare for emergencies, and
        have greater mobility and opportunities.

In the For Reflection section of this chapter is a more inclusive list by Herbert J. Gans of functions that poverty contributes to our society.

Finding our way through the tangled roots and effects is required for an accurate description of the poverty system. This is not a task just for scholars, long-range policy specialists, or program researchers. In the long run every one of us needs to become aware of the benefits and long-range costs of the system we now take for granted. Each of us needs some way to form a mental tickler file that alerts us to the many occasions when we are involved, one way or another, with the poverty sector.

FOR REFLECTION

From *Class Awareness in the United States*, by Mary Jackman and
            Robert Jackman

Pages 7-8

How then are classes best conceived? Our discussion to this point allows us to eliminate two false leads. Classes do not have to be based on a single criterion in order to become meaningful social groups, and a dichotomous division of groups is not required for conflict to take place. Once we break free of these restrictive assumptions, we can begin to view social classes in a way that is not dictated by the terms of debate originally set by Marx and Weber.

If ethnic groups can be status groups, so too can classes. Notwithstanding Weber's determined efforts to separate the concept of status groups from that of classes, there is nothing in his definition of status groups that logically precludes considering classes as social communities. Indeed, rather than undercutting the social significance of class, the substance (as opposed to the spirit) of Weber's discussion of status groups would seem to suggest classes as perfect candidates for social communities.

Like ethnic groups, these communities are loosely bounded and are based on multiple interrelated criteria. For classes, these involve configurations of economic and derivative cultural factors. Economic factors that enter the configuration include level of education, occupational prestige, job skill, security, autonomy and authority, earned income, and capital assets. These interrelated economic factors, in turn, produce variations in life styles that are expressed in patterns of consumption and cultural values. Because the definition of classes involves multiple criteria, many of which fall on continua, complete consensus about the position of group boundaries is unlikely. Nevertheless, configurations of characteristics are assembled in formal coherent social groups.

That classes are based on economic distinctions gives them a more powerful impetus for the formation of social identities than groups relying more exclusively on cultural factors for their definition (for example, ethnic groups). Economic distinctions routinely produce social differences that are readily visible and keenly experienced . . . .

If classes are social groups, then they must exist in the public consciousness. The subjective definition and interpretation of social class is an empirical problem that is critical to any theoretical approach to class. Indeed, it is this issue, more than any other, that points to the inherent limitations of traditional conceptions of class. While those conceptions have provided abstract analyses that illuminate particular features of the social structure, even casual observations of social life reveal that the population has not divided itself up neatly into owners and workers, or into those who have authority and those who do not, and so on. On the other hand we believe that the portrayal of society as lacking altogether in class awareness represents a distortion of reality that contributes little to our understanding of the dynamics of social inequality.

From *More Equality*, by Herbert J. Gans

Pages 106-113, excerpts.

"Positive Functions of Poverty"

First, the existence of poverty makes sure that "dirty" work is done. Every economy has such work: physically dirty or dangerous, temporary, dead-end and underpaid, undignified and menial jobs.

Second, the poor subsidize, indirectly or directly, many activities that benefit affluent people and institutions. For one thing, they have long supported both the consumption and the investment activities of the private economy by virtue of the low wages they receive.

Third, poverty creates jobs for a number of occupations and professions that serve the   poor, or shield the rest of the population from them. As already noted, penology would be minuscule without the poor, as would the police, since the poor provide the majority of their "clients."

Fourth, the poor buy goods that others do not want and thus prolong their economic usefulness, such as day-old bread, fruit and vegetables that would otherwise have to be thrown out, secondhand clothes, and deteriorating automobiles and buildings.

Fifth, the poor can be identified and punished as alleged or real deviants in order to uphold the legitimacy of dominant norms. . . . Whether the poor actually violate these norms more than affluent people is still open to question.

Sixth, another group of poor, described as deserving because they are disabled or suffering from bad luck, provide the rest of the population with different emotional satisfactions: they evoke compassion, pity, and charity, thus allowing those who help them to feel they are altruistic, moral, and practicing the Judeo-Christian ethic.

Seventh, the poor offer affluent people vicarious participation in the uninhibited sexual, alcoholic, and narcotic behavior in which many poor people are alleged to indulge, and which, being freed from the constraints of affluence and respectability, they are often thought to enjoy more than the middle classes.

Eighth, poverty helps to guarantee the status of those who are not poor.

Ninth, the poor also assist in the upward mobility of the non-poor.

Tenth, the poor add to the social viability of noneconomic groups. "Society" uses the poor as clients of settlement houses and charity benefits, so as to practice its public-mindedness and thus demonstrate its superiority over the *nouveaux riches* who devote themselves to

32

conspicuous consumption.

Eleventh, the poor perform several cultural functions, such as construction projects.

Twelfth, the "low" culture created for and by the poor is often adopted by the more affluent.

Thirteenth, the poor serve as symbolic constituencies and opponents for several political groups.

Fourteenth, the poor, being powerless, can be made to absorb the economic and political costs of change and growth in American society, pushed away to make more room for "progress."

Fifteenth, the poor have played an important role in shaping the American political process.

Pantheon Press, 1973, Copyright (c) Herbert J. Gans. Reprinted with permission. The author is Robert S. Lynd Professor of Sociology at Columbia University.

Describing Systemic Poverty

In 1988 The North Carolina Poverty Project invited ten academics to be a Professional Advisory Group that would assist the Project in describing "systemic poverty." A series of meetings led to adopting the following summary of their description:

Poverty refers to a set of interrelated social conditions:
* in which many businesses and other organizations pay low wages;
* in which low-paid work contributes to the benefit of other portions of the populace;
* in which people receiving low wages can afford to live only where there are concentrations of poor housing and where other dependent people are forced to live;
* in which those caught in these conditions must cope with the conse-

quences: more health problems, legal problems, social disruption;

* in which governmental and private agencies set up to serve the needy require extensive permanent bureaucratic structures to administer welfare programs;

* in which those providers of basic needs (food, education, medical care, etc.) determine what poor people can have;

* in which the needy young are exposed to a narrow range of opportunities for physical, intellectual and vocational development;

* in which social institutions established in poverty areas have limited resources

* in which needy areas receive minimal general community services; and

* in which this portion of the population, with little influence or power, is looked down upon with disdain and blame.

Group members:

Economics: Prof. Thomas E. Till, St. Andrews Presbyterian College

Education: Dean Charles R. Coble, East Carolina University

Ethics: Prof. Harmon Smith, Duke University

Health: Prof. C. Arden Miller, UNC-Chapel Hill

History: Prof. Melton A. McLaurin, UNC-Wilmington

Law: Mr. Richard M. Taylor, Jr., Legal Services of North Carolina

Political Science: Prof. Sheridan W. Johns, Duke University

Psychology: Prof. M. David Galinsky, UNC-Chapel Hill

Social Work: Prof. Andrew W. Dobelstein, UNC-Chapel Hill

Sociology: Prof. Robert Davis, NC A&T State University

———

In a series of workshops conducted by the North Carolina Poverty Project in 1994 participants from seven states adopted:

Causes of Poverty

Diagnosis

Diagnosing the basic causes of poverty requires a recognition that the term "poverty" is used in two very different ways:

1. When poverty refers to conditions under which individuals and families live, diagnosing its cause(s) can be particular and the ways to overcome their condition can be direct and obvious.

2. However, when poverty refers to an aspect of a socio-economic system which requires that some people be poor, diagnosing its causes involves a very different arena, and overcoming those causes is a much more complex task.

"Poverty" in the first sense expresses a common perspective on the reality of needy individuals and families and underlies the approach of numerous public and private agencies struggling to help the poor.

"Poverty" in the second sense expresses a different perspective. The most explicit evidence of the second reality is that among the poor in this society are many who work but whose pay is below what it costs them to live. According to the U.S. Census Bureau 8,994,000 men and women worked but had incomes below the poverty line in 1991.

Because society depends upon such people for tasks essential to the whole socio-economic system, their poverty is systemic. It is ingrained in the structures and practices of the institutions which maintain the taken-for-granted patterns of our common life.

The devastating impact of poverty on individuals and the society as a whole is an inescapable reality, but seldom is it addressed in terms of its basic causes. Why?

A common assumption is that people are poor because of their own inadequacies; so no further examination of "cause" is needed. This view assists in reinforcing systemic poverty.

Others, who share the cultural value of individualism, hold a somewhat similar view of the poor, based on the idea that working one's way out of poverty is the responsibility of each individual, and therefore questions of some other cause are not raised.

Also, many people prefer to concentrate on the immense resources and opportunities for millions provided by this socio/economic/political system and seem to assume that all that is needed is further expansion of that system. They are reluctant to dwell on the possible negative aspects of benefits: such as, chemistry provides blessings but also pollutes our aquifers, or that "economic development" can also increase poverty.

The benefits of charity deflect attention from the systemic causes of poverty. When the billions of dollars spent on thousands of programs for the poor is considered as charity and a social virtue, little attention needs to be given to questions of why poverty still persists in a multi-trillion-dollar economy.

Giving to charity is seen as a virtue, but depending on charity as a vice. In this way benevolence directs attention to the character of the poor rather than to the causes of their poverty.

The result of inattention to the causes of poverty is that poverty is taken for granted. "The poor ye shall have with you always" becomes a sufficient explanation of poverty.

Poverty and Poor

Biblical references to the poor could not anticipate the modern socio-economic system in which poverty has become an essential element. In contemporary society individuals and families are poor for a variety of reasons. But why a family is poor may differ from the reasons why poverty is systemic.

Those who are willing to address causes are often confused by the use of "poor" and "poverty" to refer to the same reality. One evidence of confusion has been the federal government's "poverty line" which implies that families with incomes below that line are "in poverty" while those with incomes above the line are no longer poor for they are "out of poverty." Were that the case, it would mean that in 1993 a family of four with an income of $14,500 was no longer poor in a country with a per capita income, then, of $18,841.

The "poverty line" has been widely used in academic and statistical studies, business decisions and government policies, but it has little to do either with what it costs to live or with what "poor" means to most people. When public health nurses were asked what annual income their families of four would need in order to no longer feel poor, their answers averaged $44,000 a year. Newspaper editors' answers averaged

$47,000. "Poor" is a relative term.

A second confusion has to do with the common assumption that the words "poor" and "poverty" are simply economic terms. While poverty refers to economic realities it, like all other economic ideas, expresses cultural values and relationships. It is produced and perpetuated by the choices and beliefs of those who take our inherited institutional structures and practices for granted as acceptable cultural norms.

Culture

Cultural ideas, beliefs, and assumptions reinforce each other. Among the dominant themes that characterize the culture of the United States are work, freedom, equality, individualism, charity, and competition. Although deeply rooted in our past, present commitments to them shape the common life of this country. They are grounds for the opportunities and benefits referred to as "the American Dream."

What is very difficult for many to recognize is that these valued ideas and beliefs also provide the grounds for perpetuating poverty. Claims that "the poor subsidize us all," or that "charity can be unjust" are not particularly welcomed. But cultural values are not absolutes. Individualism when unrestrained, destroys community, and unlimited freedom for some denies freedom to others. A critical examination of cultural values is necessary if people of this society are to understand the causes of "systemic poverty" and be able to overcome its blight.

Freedom for individuals to develop their natural gifts, pursue their interests, believe as they wish, and choose the direction of their lives is not only an ideal, it is a reality for many people in this society. Institutional structures, laws, and community practices sustain opportunities for individual freedom from which the whole society benefits, but they also lead to insulation of the non-poor from the poor.

Growing up in a community where pay for the only jobs available is too low to support a decent level of living, where houses, schools, churches, health services, and recreational facilities are all inadequate, the young have little freedom to escape that condition.

Understanding the way cultural values function in church, business,

and government for the benefit of some and the handicap of others, provides the changed perspective needed if systemic poverty is to be overcome.

Therefore, examining the causes of ingrained poverty requires exploring the way cultural values of freedom, equality, individualism, charity, and competition are related to another value, work.

Work

"Work" holds both a distinctive and a curious place in the beliefs, attitudes, and commitments of this society. In different contexts work can be what gives meaning to life, or it provides support for other more meaningful activities, or it is seen as a civic responsibility. For some it is punishment.

These beliefs and attitudes about work involve poverty in two ways: status and dependence.

What workers are paid reflects the cultural status accorded to various kinds of work. High status is given to entertainment, handling money, surgical skill, management, and white-collar positions. Low status is accorded to taking care of children, writing poetry, teaching skills, preparing food, housework, and blue-collar jobs.

Status also relates to gender. Work men do has higher status, and therefore better pay, than work women do (often when women have the same jobs as men), distinctions which relate neither to whether the work is essential, nor to its morality. While work is often given high social value and is expected of the poor, it is not similarly expected of the wealthy.

Status accorded certain kinds of work is built into institutional structures and is sustained by laws, religious views, educational procedures, and business practices, thus perpetuating poverty regardless of who does those jobs.

In addition to common assumptions about the kinds of work they do, a common attitude is that the poor are a social handicap, depending on society for food, clothing, shelter, and medical care. Seldom is there a balancing realization of the extent to which this society depends upon the poor to subsidize the non-poor.

Millions of men and women work at essential tasks, fulfilling what society expects of them, yet their income is below the poverty line. And the poverty line is far below the cost of living. In consequence, these essential workers have to live in poor housing in danger of crime and drugs, are often hungry, have more medical problems than the non-poor, cannot afford health insurance, have more legal problems, cannot save for emergencies or for their old age and are looked down on with disdain. Negative attitudes toward the poor on the part of so many in this society, evident in common stereotypes, play a strong supporting role in the cultural causes of systemic poverty.

Structures

Contending that poverty is built into our socio-cultural system is not to place blame on particular individuals or sectors. It is to recognize that the character of a culture is "institutionalized" in many organizations by which society carries on its essential activities. Companies, schools, churches, clubs, political parties, associations all have roles to play in society and all are involved with the poor.

Perpetuation of poverty is structural, and is maintained by those many institutions of the community and the state. Those who are isolated from the experience of being poor do not realize that because the poor live with deprivation of many kinds theirs is a "communal (rather than a familial) cycle of poverty."

Ideas of freedom and individual rights, with deep roots in the nation's history, shape each of our institutions. That shaping is particularly evident in schools. The availability of schooling for all is a national commitment. Where it works as intended schooling can provide an opportunity for individual self-discovery and development of gifts.

Yet in the way schools, churches, and universities promote individualism they share with other institutions in reinforcing ingrained structures and practices which take poverty for granted. When competition is emphasized more than community, when the over-whelming problems of poverty are left out of the curriculum, and when states allow "savage inequality" between schools in poor and affluent communities (as described by Jonathan Kozol), students who start out in setting of deprivation do not have equal opportunity.

In summary:

Systemic poverty is reinforced when cultural values of freedom, equality, individualism, charity, and competition are interpreted by the non-poor to justify the resulting limitations of opportunities and benefits to the working poor and their children.

Systemic poverty is perpetuated when dependence upon such workers is taken for granted in the structures and practices of institutions in society.

Overcoming systemic poverty in a community or state will be possible when its responsible leaders are helped to gain a new perspective that recognizes both the long-range dangers in continuing the present approach and the long-range benefits to the community if needed changes are made now.

Addressing the following issues is basic:

1. Confusion growing from different uses of the words "poverty" and "poor": help people see the invalidity of an arbitrary poverty line and how it misrepresents the problem; bring into the open the fact that what poverty means to people varies widely; and work on obtaining some consensus on what constitutes a decent level of living.

2. Corroding influences of negative attitudes toward the poor: explore their religious roots; expose stereotypes of many kinds and the tendency to generalize from limited experiences; and show how negative views of welfare function to deprive the needy of benefits to which they are entitled.

3. The way poverty is ingrained in organizations to which people are committed: help participants and leaders see that involvement with poverty differs among various kinds of organizations; consider the civic responsibilities of organizations, not only of individuals; and specific steps that each organization can take toward changing its policies and practices.

4. Organizational use of the working poor: recognize that there are many kinds of employers who need not be bound to pay the lowest possible

wages; appreciate the extent to which their organizations depend upon the poor for essential services; see how welfare for the working poor becomes an indirect subsidy for their employers; and face the ethical implications of forcing people to depend on welfare to supplement their pay in order to live.

5. The geography of poverty: consider the damaging impact of the geography of poverty in urban ghettos and rural areas; see how the cycle of poverty relates more to community than to family; and face the need for long-range planning that will overcome the increasingly dangerous divide between the poor and the affluent in this society.

6. At a deeper level it is necessary to recognize that poverty is an issue of human community, and therefore it has to do with the uses of power; that power shapes relations between the haves and the have-nots; that the basic social issue is justice which involves the limitations of power; and that every decision of a society has inescapable ethical dimensions.

Failure to adhere to the most fundamental values of humanity has resulted in persistent and systemic poverty in our society. It is our conviction that this is not fated to be. Change is possible.

With insights from this diagnosis, the assistance of a new perspective, and clarification of issues to be considered, the next step is to develop fresh and creative processes in each power sector which engage its leaders in the task of planning, promoting, and then adopting policies and programs that will overcome systemic poverty.

The 16 participants in the workshops were from Alabama, Georgia, Kentucky, North Carolina, Pennsylvania, South Carolina, and Tennessee.

Chapter 4

THEIR WORLD

America's social arrangement produces benefits for employers and the public at large, but it produces quite different effects for the poor. The list is long:

* The poor often must pay more for groceries and other purchases because they live far from large stores and have to buy at small isolated shops. Walking means going to the closest market, not the least expensive. Many cannot afford a car and must use taxis, often having to pay extra for each bag of groceries. Those who depend on bus service to the grocery store limit their purchases to what they can carry.

* Most poor are unable to borrow money because interest rates are higher for them than for the non-poor, and sometimes the cost of insurance is added to the loan. In other words, immediate needs often force the poor to make bad economic choices when the roof leaks, the refrigerator dies, the purse is stolen, or the car needs new tires. The poor have no capacity to save up for "the rainy day."

* The poor are more likely to live near garbage dumps, chemical plants, and toxic-emitting industries.

* Those living in poor areas of cities are more exposed to violence, drug selling, antisocial behavior, and danger.

* Local and state taxes vary across the country, but most poor pay a higher percent of their income for taxes than do the affluent.

* No matter where the poor live they can not afford on-ramps to the information highway, and thus their children do not begin life on a level playing field in preparing for new kinds of technical jobs.

* Although cities attract rich lodes of artistic, intellectual, and cultural opportunities, all of these are usually beyond the reach of the poor.

The employed poor have additional handicaps:

* Many jobs have mixed schedules or are at meal times so that poor families can seldom have regular meals together.

* Most jobs do not provide for pensions or vacation time so the poor are often immobilized and cannot experience the stimulation of travel in a society whose non-poor are increasingly mobile.

* Increasingly new jobs are located in the suburbs resulting in limited and expensive transportation for workers from poor ghettos.

These handicaps are listed one by one, but most poor families confront them simultaneously. The poor can agree with Shakespeare that when troubles come "they come not single spies but in battalions." They are daily experiences shared by those who have to live in enclaves of the poor.

Separate geographies means that the adults whom children of the poverty sector meet and watch are people with low status and low-paying jobs. Children of the poor have no exposure to people with interesting upper level jobs. They know about working conditions only from discussions of their parents, play only with other children of the poor, have less access to parks and playgrounds and, particularly in cities, generally go to poor schools.

Much attention has been focused on contrasts in the schooling of the poor and the non-poor. Jonathan Kozol gives dramatic accounts of city after city where decrepit, run-down old buildings house overcrowded classrooms with inadequate equipment, antiquated text books and inferior libraries that serve the children of the poor; while just blocks away up-to-date buildings, small classes, and ample facilities are provided for children of the non-poor. He calls these gaps between the two worlds, "savage inequalities."[3]

Perhaps more important than the contrasts in student expenditures and the quality of facilities is the fact that most teachers of poor children are from the non-poor world. Having grown up in non-poor families and communities, and attended non-poor colleges and universities, these teachers find it difficult (even when they try) to understand the views of the world which have shaped their students.

Geographical separation between poor and non-poor areas of cities (and often of rural areas as well) and the lack of easy access to medical services contributes to sharp differences in the health situation of the poor. The poor do not have family doctors or dentists; they have to depend on emergency rooms for even minor problems, such as colds or earaches. Without preventive care or early treatment provided by a family doctor, the poor are likely to become sicker and then with more serious complications they turn to hospitals or clinics where they often have to explain their problems to a different doctor each time.

Because the poor are constricted geographically, their troubles become amplified by the experiences of communal stress and danger. And because the poor are not able to accumulate resources to meet such troubles, they must always turn to one or another agency and ask for charity.

These many factors become pressures shaping the "world" of one-third (not one-fourth as claimed by studies based on the "poverty line") of the children in this country. For millions of children the lenses through which they view the world around them, and thereby view themselves and their families, reflect those constant pressures and deprivations.

There is one exception, however, in the limited exposures of the poor: television. Now a three-year-old child can control his or her exposure to the world beyond the home.

That child, and siblings or parents, can turn on the TV to any channel they want and watch the world outside. For poor children the broader and more open their view of the world, the deeper is their awareness of being closed in by a crowd of handicaps and pressures, and therefore the greater their awareness of the gap between their world and the outside world.

Parental experience of the gap can be quite different from that of their children, and often parents seek to shield their children from the doubled pressures they encounter daily.

The employed poor are in the middle. Their world overlaps with ours. Every job they do involves direct relation with the non-poor world, whether in trying to work out problems of transportation, setting up a work schedule, cooking and cleaning in lovely homes they could never afford, serving expensive meals to diners who can easily pay for what is far beyond the waiter's means, or taking orders from a boss who assumes that workers are his or her servants. This is a life of perpetual servitude in which workers know that their role is to make things comfortable for others, and that what they are doing is essential to the system on which both poor and non-poor depend for their living.

While their work life is among the non-poor, when they go home they are back among their neighbors who are not working and therefore are poorer. The effect of these very different demands and pressures with which they have to contend makes despair a constant companion, feeds a conviction that the world is unfair, and gives continuing assurance that they and their neighbors are in the enclave because they have no power structure by which to attain a decent life.

Lord Acton wrote that "power tends to corrupt," but Mechal Lerner contends that being powerless also corrupts. He writes,

> Powerlessness corrupts in a very direct way: It changes, transforms, and distorts us. It makes us different from how we would otherwise want to be. We look at our world and our own behavior, and we tell ourselves that although we really aren't living the lives we want to live, there is nothing we can do about it. We are powerless.[4]

And later,

> The basic fact is this: American society is a class-dominated society. What that amounts to is: (1.) A small number of people have vast economic power while the overwhelming majority has almost no power in the economic realm. The few million who own the vast resources of our society get to shape the basic decisions of production, employment, and how resources will be used. (2.) Economic power gives that small group a huge amount of political power. . . . (3.) Most institutions of our society accept this framework as given, and then try to serve the interests of those with power.[5]

A serious consequence of the separate geographies which mark the landscape of this society is that most non-poor individuals, as well as non-poor institutions, are comfortable with this arrangement. It is as though we believe that it is appropriate for the poor to live among the poor; that relative property values justify this separation, and that people whom we think of as inadequate will feel more at home among others like themselves. Being comfortable with things as they are is one indication that the non-poor (except for staff of social service agencies) know very little about how the poor live or about conditions in poverty-stricken enclaves.

Since the poor know much more about us than we know about them, they are in constant discomfort with things as they are. The main thing the poor learn early is that they are deprived and powerless. They see it all around them; they hear it from their pals and parents; they see it in some television ads and sit-coms. The contrast between a world of comfort and their own world is always central in the consciousness of poor people.

Most of us have been shaped by the pressures, attitudes, values, and expectations of the world around us without having to confront realities that contrast with our own. From early childhood onward, the shaping influences of our world seldom include the fact that we are privileged. Who would tell us that? Not our parents, not our schools, and not the television set.

Most of us take our opportunities for granted. For those in positions of social control the gap between their world and the world of the poor is seen as valid. A key component of the poverty system is our lack of knowledge about the many ways we benefit from the labor of the poor. We take their labor and the fruits of their labor for granted. This perpetuates their poverty.

A principal reason we do not know about the realities of being poor, and the consequences of these realities for society, is that such things have not been included in our formal or non-formal education. It is important to note the near total absence of the study of poverty from the curricula of universities and colleges.

One of the barriers to the study of poverty is our ambiguity about the much vaunted value of "work." The emphasis on "work" by political leaders of the 1990s does not assure those who are working that they will be treated any differently from the poor who do not work.

Four different relations to work can be identified among the poor:

those who cannot work,

those who could work if adequate training were available,

those who do work on their own, and

those who are employed.

Under the present system all of these are required to seek from public or private welfare agencies, assistance with food, housing, transportation, medical services, and child care.

We may proclaim that work gives meaning to life, but the meaning it has for us is very different from its meaning for those who make life comfortable for us. They gain no social benefit from being employed. To be called the working class is not an expression of honor. To be identified as a blue collar worker usually implies disdain. These are terms used by the non-poor who do not "work." We are professionals, we are managers, we occupy positions. We are identified by our function in society rather than by the actual tasks we perform.

Headlines keep attacking those who are not working but fail to acknowledge that low status jobs mean low pay. Our social setup does not offer the employed poor any escape from deprivation and danger. Those at the bottom, who provide services without which no society or institution can survive, are consigned to multiple individual and social indignities.

One of those indignities is the demeaning way the employed poor are processed as they try to meet needs beyond what they can afford from their wages. Although they are working at essential jobs, when troubles strike they must go to the Department of Social Services, Community Action, or some other crisis assistance agency, fill out forms, explain their financial situation, and meet fixed regulations which determine whether or not they will get bus coupons, furnace oil, food, or clothes.

In this demeaning process, non-poor persons determine what the poor will receive. Agency staff members making such decisions may be caring and deeply concerned for the welfare of their clients, but they are constrained by state and federal requirements adopted by other non-poor people whose good intentions are another demonstration of their inability to understand the daily realities of the poor.

Even more demeaning is our common concern about how the poor depend on us even as we fail to admit how we depend on them. Typical of this view is a book by June Axinn and Mark Stern, *Dependency and Poverty*, in which they analyze many kinds of dependency of the poor, but they never consider the numerous ways the rest of us depend on the poor.[6] Their views typify not only our common insensitivity to how unfair it is to expect the poor to serve us when we pay them less than it costs them to live, but also the strangely inconsistent views of work in our culture.

The poor work because they need to eat, have some place to live, and take care of their children in decency. They work for the same reasons we do.

Chapter 5

WHAT WE DO

Those of us who are not poor have employed two interrelated processes to maintain the poverty sector in our social arrangement. We do so because the arrangement benefits all of us. Poverty is perpetuated by what we do *for* the poor as well as what we do *to* the poor.

For the Poor

As concerned people of this country have learned about the consequences of poverty their consciences have prompted them to develop numberless enterprises for dealing with that human blight.

During our lifetime there have been two periods of engrossing attention devoted to dealing with the poor. One was prompted by the Great Depression, the other by the Civil Rights movement. They generated the New Deal of the 1930s and the War on Poverty of the 1960s.

Some programs in the New Deal provided paying jobs to hundreds of thousands of people who worked on projects of lasting value to the whole society. Such programs are now generally opposed by many politicians and, probably, by much of the public at large. But the programs addressed the structure and system by which we function.

The most significant was the minimum-wage law which has from time to time been adjusted. At first the minimum wage was sufficient to provide a decent level of living for workers. However, Congress frequently neglected to raise the minimum wage in keeping with the rising cost of living. Seven years of such neglect in the 1980s forced the employed poor to depend more and more upon charity to meet basic needs.

Opposition to raising the minimum wage is vigorous whenever it is proposed. Some in business believe that there should be no limits at all on the market as arbiter of wages. However, there has not been a strong move to eliminate this federal government adjustment of the system.

The War on Poverty established by the Economic Opportunity Act of 1964 incorporated a broad range of programs including the Neighborhood Youth Corps which included a Work-Study program; the Urban and Rural Community Action which included Adult Basic Education and Head Start; a Rural Loan Program which included programs for migrant workers and dairy farmers; the Small Business Administration; the Work Experience Program; and an Office of Economic Opportunity to direct the set of programs. To assist state and local agencies Vista was also established.

A second feature addressing the system is Legal Services, which has joint federal-private support. Repeated attempts were made in the 1980s to withdraw federal support of this program but in each instance Congress voted its continuation, while also cutting back on the amount of federal funding. Legal Services continue to be strongly supported by bar associations on both the national and state levels.

Legal Services was organized on a national basis in 1965 by the Office of Economic Opportunity to provide legal services to the poor. The program constituted a change in the system and was devoted to protecting the legal rights of the poor, but the limitations on what they can do are very obvious. In much of the nation there is a lawyer for every 700 people. Legal Services can provide only one lawyer for every 7,000 poor people. Administrative and legislative limitations on Legal Services' time and resources makes it very difficult for the state to assure "equal justice under the law."

The third attack on systemic poverty has been private, the union movement. For many years unions were able to organize workers and, using both negotiations and strikes, to obtain a range of benefits including more adequate incomes for their members. Through the exercise of political power, unions have been able to obtain various kinds of assistance by the federal Department of Labor on other objectives such as safer work places and fairer treatment of workers.

Each of these three approaches produced mountains of literature, acres of bureaucracies to conduct the many federal, state, and local governmental programs, and innumerable private agencies conducting programs to help the poor. Paralleling the many service agencies have been specialized advocacy groups, political action movements, and a wide range of cultural and media attention devoted to the poverty situation, both pro and con. All of these activities were accompanied and followed by statistical studies and critical evaluations that piled up more books, reports, and other documents.

Kevin Phillips has quoted Representative Green of Oregon commenting, in 1969, that "probably our most enduring monument to the problem of poverty has been the creation of a poverty industry. There are more than 100 companies in Washington, D.C. alone which specialize in studying and evaluating the poor and the programs that serve them."[6]

The American penchant for "doing something" has found expression in a wide range of organizations set up, not only in Washington but across the country, to meet human needs, including the needs of the poor. Some of these organizations had been active from long before the Depression, but their number continues to increase. The latest directory of community assistance available in any cosmopolitan area probably lists a thousand or more health and human service programs. Perhaps the most significant private programs were Food Banks coordinated by the national Second Harvest office, and Habitat for Humanity, a distinctive effort initiated by former President Jimmy Carter.

We all know about government programs but few of us are aware of how wide the range of attempts to help the poor have been. Even those of us who have participated in the efforts of private agencies, social clubs, community organizations, emergency and crisis services, or private advocacy, seldom have an opportunity to become familiar with the total scope of these activities.

A second important development has been the "spin offs" of governmental programs, such as Community Action which, from the beginning, was to be a joint public-private effort. It is interesting, and significant, that so many of the government-supported programs went far beyond the federally designated programs by developing an amazing variety of "spin offs." An account of the amplification of services by Community Action in just one state is included in the For Reflection section of this chapter.

Many who shared in these efforts were simply responding to obvious needs of the poor and assuming that "the poor will be with us always." For others the objective, more ambitious and optimistic, was to overcome the blight. Creative scholars at the University of Wisconsin in Madison, who in 1963 organized the Institute for Research on Poverty, thought that poverty could be ended in nine years. At a 25th anniversary meeting they amused each other in recalling that false hope.

We recognize that those huge efforts, public and private, have helped meet critical needs of the poor for food, clothing, shelter, and medical care. Concern for the poor has been genuine, but too often the efforts were based on the assumption that the causes were personal, that is, blighted childhood, inadequate experience, limited education, parental sloth, physical and mental handicaps. That assumption limited the efforts to amelioration, but even those have failed because they were not intended to overcome systemic poverty.

New Deal and War on Poverty progams were not designed to address poverty's systemic causes. Why attempts to address the systemic causes of poverty generated limited support poses a puzzle. Why, while depending on the poor for so many services, are there such widespread negative assumptions about them? It is not easy to explain. As the King of Siam said, "It is a puzzlement."

Is it because we all depend on the poor and resent having to be dependent on people we usually shun? Is it because some of us were once poor and since moving up we look down on those who have not done likewise? Is it because we need to maintain our self-esteem by being assured that we are better than others? Is it because we gave a turkey to a poor family last Thanksgiving and they did not thank us? Or is it because we believe, along with many of our forefathers, that being poor is a just punishment for their immorality? How do you interpret the public mood on these things?

Of course there are other attitudes flowing in our common stream of social awareness. Some people tend to romanticize the poor, as Charles Kuralt did from time to time in his CBS Series, "On the Road." Others think that being poor can be used to discipline behavior. For centuries in Western culture, poverty has been held as a virtue, and taking a vow of poverty a religious duty. In this often moralistic society, charity can walk hand in hand with harsh expectations.

To the Poor

It is important for the non-poor majority to recognize that these mixed and conflicting attitudes toward the poor are involved in shaping what we do *to* them as well as what we are doing *for* them.

While numerous public and private social service programs express positive concerns for the poor, they are being conducted within a common atmosphere of blaming the poor for their condition. And that common atmosphere is a response to the obvious. Of course there are poor people who cheat, lie, are lazy, want to be taken care of, don't want to work, don't keep up their yards, and abuse their children. But we have to admit that such behavior is not limited to the poor. It can be found on all levels of society.

So why does such behavior bother us more when it is by the poor than when by the non-poor? Why do we train more police for street crime than for white-collar "suite" crime? Is it because some of our taxes go to help those poor and we resent it? Or is it because we think such behavior is more prominent among the poor? If that is what we think what proof do we have? Well, this may lead us to part of the answer.

We, the non-poor, are very dependent on common shared beliefs and assumptions about the poor. Because we and they occupy different worlds the common bridge between us is stereotypes.

It is often assumed that stereotypes are unfair, even though the term has no such connotation in its original printing context. While stereotypes often do misrepresent conditions it is important to recognize that, whether negative or positive, they perform significant functions.

Stereotypes are a sort of growing vine which helps hold a group or community together in approving or objecting to the actions of others. Or they are a kind of thermometer, indicating the level of attitudes and feelings in the body politic. Carefully studied they provide a measure of a group's knowledge or ignorance of other groups in their communities.

An important function of stereotypes is their exposure of assumptions about the causes of conditions to which they refer. Stereotypes seldom apply to institutions, they apply to persons. They serve to express a common assumption that the cause of poverty is personal rather than social.

One of the most shopworn stereotypes floating through our society is of the woman wearing a mink coat driving to the grocery store in her Cadillac to buy T-bone steaks with food stamps. This is seldom used to indicate malfeasance on the part of a social service agency which provided those food stamps without checking on their use. It reflects an assumption that those who get food stamps are cheaters.

However, when such stereotypes are employed by legislators as a guide to policy they function either to explain what has been done or to rationalize actions taken.

And of course, stereotypes often provide abundant excuses for inaction on a social issue. "What is the point of trying when we have to work with people like that?"

A stereotype is a generalization based on a particular encounter or series of encounters. Our stereotypes are second-hand ideas, beliefs, opinions, or attitudes formed in the normal round of social connections. Most of them are derived from encounters, or assumed encounters, of others.

Since we are all part of social bodies larger than the immediate family there is no way for each of us to have a direct experience of all the other individuals or groups that constitute our local, regional, national, or global communities. We function largely by generalizations. These inform our likes and dislikes, our approval or disapproval. They are a kind of predisposition of attitude, shaping our expectations when we do encounter those "others." They are a normal form of human social relation. And they have an effect on how we vote.

Unfortunately, this normal human process functions too frequently as an explanation of conditions rather than as a serious careful diagnosis. It becomes a public judgment by the majority upon those whom we know very little about. One device employed by those who seek to overcome the gap between the two worlds has been to organize exchanges by which the non-poor have direct and extended opportunities to learn more about the poor.

A doctor and his family arrange to live for a week with a poor family. An affluent church and a poor church agree to exchange some members for a year. A few poor children are sent to a summer camp for a week or so. These efforts can provide significant benefits for individuals, families, and congregations. However, they do not address the deeper issue.

The deep moralistic strain in American culture often generates bountiful "letters to the editor" about how others should behave. Perhaps we all feel the urge to write such a letter when we witness or hear about behavior we deplore. It can apply to all levels of society, but it is particularly destructive when it focuses on the people at the bottom.

In the For Reflection section of this chapter is a report by Derrick Z. Jackson which shows the depth of public hostility toward the poor, particularly when it involves race.

But Herbert J. Gans goes even deeper. In *The War Against the Poor* he gives a careful step-by-step description of how the idea of "underclass," first employed as an economic category, has been transformed into a "behavioral" category. A summary of that transformation is in the For Reflection section of this chapter.

Common and popular views about the poor have deep roots in major features of the "American character," for they have grown out of the American experience. They have been built into our inherited institutional structures and practices and taken for granted as cultural norms.

Among the dominant themes that characterize the culture of the United States are freedom (particularly on the "frontier"), equality, individualism, competition, and work. Although rooted in our past, present commitments to them shape the common life of the country.

Currently there is a nation-wide preoccupation, as we have noted, which elevates "work" above the others.

What is very difficult for many to recognize is that these values, ideas, and beliefs help perpetuate poverty, particularly when they are held as absolutes. Individualism when unrestrained destroys community, and becomes corrupt when it holds that individual effort is the primary determinant of affluence or poverty.

Similarly, unlimited freedom for some denies freedom to others. When these "cultural values" are institutionalized in laws and social practices they sustain opportunities for individuals, but they also lead to isolation of the poor from the non-poor and damage both government and private efforts to address this social blight.

Consequences

The consequence of our present social structure is a dilemma. It arises when what we do for the poor results in what we do to the poor. It is a troubling puzzle deeply ingrained in the total American experience. We need to recognize that the present generation did not design the socio-cultural system which we now share. Those who have studied past efforts to deal with poverty offer valuable insights for our consideration of both personal and civic responsibilities. They show that not only our individual views but also our institutional structures have deep roots. Reexamining our views and structures requires a serious effort to deepen and broaden our understanding of America's poverty system. Such understanding is needed before we can develop appropriate solutions.

But seeking such solutions returns us to the dilemma that the immense expenditures and the multitudes of programs based on serious study by thousands of scholars have not overcome poverty.

Pointing out the gap between the poor and the non-poor, or noting the common stereotypes which attempt to explain it, provides no guidance for bridging that damaging gap. Our very American spontaneous response to obvious need traps us in the paradox of commitments which inherently conflict. We want straightforward, plain, workable solutions. But our cultural puzzle is oxymoronic. We do not see that what ameliorates also perpetuates, that in volunteering to serve meals at a soup kitchen we are giving and taking in the same act. The paradox is personal for we should thank the hungry family for coming to the soup kitchen so we can have an opportunity to be virtuous. But the paradox is ingrained in our social structures as well. We often have very ambivalent views about taxes, when we see them as both a civic duty and a benevolence to those on welfare. Seldom do we admit that often we are recipients of a tax structure which provides welfare for the non-poor.

Resolving the puzzle requires clarifying what we mean by poverty and that involves making a distinction between those who are poor because of personal inadequacies and those who are poor because they are caught in a system which demands their labor but denies them an adequate income. We who are not poor are the ones who create this dilemma by our choices based on our views and beliefs. The resolution requires: recognition of the cause, a living wage for bottom workers, and sharing by all of us who are not poor in meeting the needs of those who cannot work and those who for many legitimate reasons are not working.

* * * * *

FOR REFLECTION

Most of us have difficulty grasping the tremendous number of agencies, programs, and services for the poor now functioning in this society. Community Action was part of the War on Poverty and it functions in all states. The following list illustrates the extended scope of that agency in just one state.

From *Community Action in North Carolina*, published by The North Carolina Poverty Project, 1993.

Thirty-six Community Action agencies serve most of the one hundred counties in the state with a variety of what they call "current programs."

These programs are administered by the Community Action staff and typically include such activities as: Community Service Block Grants, Dependent Care, Drop Out Program, Community College subsidies, Head Start, Foster Grandparents, Family Planning, Housing: to standard, Nutrition: home delivery to the aged, Retired Service volunteers, Stop Teen Pregnancy, Transportation, Vocational Education, Weatherization. In addition to the many regular programs, most of the Community Action agencies have encouraged an even wider range of "spinoffs," as listed below.

Alamance County Community Services Agency, 8 current programs
Blue Ridge Community Action, 19 current programs
Blue Ridge Opportunity Commission, 12 current programs and spinoffs:
    Allegheny County Planning Committee
    Catherine Barber Memorial Homeless Shelter
    National Health Service Corps Project
    We Care Planning, Inc.
    Wilkes Community Action Committee
Carteret Community Action, 14 current programs and spinoffs:
    Economic Developmental Council
    High School Drop-Outs
    Job Corps Recruiting
Charlotte Area Fund, 7 current programs and spinoffs:
    Concentrated Employment Program
    Head Start
    Hot Lunch Program
    Legal Aid Society
    Metrolina Food Bank
    Neighborhood Youth Corps
Choanoke Area Development Association, 14 current programs and spinoffs:
    Choanoke Public Transit Authority
    Chore Services
    Low-Income Energy Assistance Program
    Summer Food Service/Recreation Program

Telephone Reassurance Network/Senior Citizens

Food Pantry

Income Tax Assistance

Cumberland Community Action Program, 9 current programs

Davidson County Community Action, 2 current programs

Duplin Onslow Pender Consolidated Human Services, 13 current programs and spinoffs:

Coastal Growers Cucumber Corporation

Council on Aging

Feeder Pig Project

Meals on Wheels

Outs-Onslow United Transit Systems

Economic Improvement Council, 7 current programs and spinoffs:

Economic Development Program

Family Planning

Food & Nutrition Program

Low-Income Energy Assistance Program

Manpower Program

Senior Citizens Program

Experiment In Self-Reliance, 14 current programs and spinoffs:

Early Childhood Development Center

Farm Program

Food Bank of N.W. North Carolina

Head Start

Legal Aid

Neighborhood Justice Center

TRANS-AID

Youth Cultural Program

Four-County Community Action, 9 current programs

Four Square Community Action, 7 current programs and spinoffs:

Mountain Skill Crafts Cooperative

Southwestern N.C. Craft and Farmers' Market

Franklin-Vance-Warren Opportunity, 10 current programs and spinoffs:

Green Hill Manor

Green Hill Village

Kerr Area Regional Transportation System
N.C. Senior Citizens Federation
Franklin-Vance-Warren Housing of Warren County
Warren County Self-Help Homeownership Program
Warren County Rental Assistance Program
Gaston Community Action, 7 current programs
Green Lamp, 15 current programs and spinoffs:
   Crisis Intervention
   Foster Grandparents
   Weatherization
   Women, Infants & Children
Guilford County Community Action Program, 8 current programs
Head Start of New Hanover, 5 current programs
I Care (Iredell Community Action, Research & Evaluation), 9 current
   programs and spinoffs:
   Ruthies Day Care
   Senior Feeding Program
   Women, Infants and Children Program
Johnson-Lee Community Action, 7 current programs and spinoffs:
   Alcohol Recovery Program
   Drug Action Committee
   Energy Crisis Program
   Juvenile Restitution Program
   Home Health
   Medical Transit Service
   Migrant Head Start
   Nutrition Program for the Elderly
   Project Pride
   Senior Citizens Clubs
Orange-Chatham Community Action, 6 current programs and spinoffs:
   North State Legal Services
   Orange-Chatham Home Repair, Inc.
   NC Rural Communities Assistance Project
   Chatham County Housing Authority
   Siler City Housing Corporation

Orange County Department of Aging

Orange County Community Development Corporation

Macon Program For Progress, 13 current programs and spinoffs:

Mountain Federal Credit Union

Maco Crafts

Macon Citizens Enterprises

Macon Housing Development Corporation

Martin County Community Action, 8 current programs and spinoffs:

Emergency Medical Assistance

Homemaker Program

Human Resource Development

Nurses Aide Program

On the Job Training

Planned Assurance College Education

Teacher Assistance Program

Mountain Projects, 11 current programs and spinoffs:

Balsam Originals

Family Planning

Meals on Wheels

Tutorial Program

Western Economic Development Organization

Nash-Edgecombe Economic Development, 16 current programs and spinoffs:

Job Corps Recruitment

GED Classes

Home Repair Loans

Community Organizations

Temporary Transportation/Day Care Services

Economic Development

Home Day Care

Family Development Centers

Adopt-A-Poverty-Family Project

Operation Breakthrough, 6 current programs and spinoffs:

Russell Memorial Child Care Center

United Durham Community Development Corporation

62

Opportunity Corporation of Madison-Buncombe Counties, 6 current
   programs
Salisbury-Rowan Community Service Council, 13 current programs and
   spinoffs:
   Aging Program
   Clothes Closet
   Urban Mass Transit
Sandhills Community Action Program, 11 current programs and spinoffs:
   Adult Basic Educatioon
   Criminal Justice
   Emergency Food
   Family Planning
   Job Training (CETA)
   Head Start
   Job Mobile
   Job Training
   Neighborhood Youth Corps
   Small Business Assistance
   Dial-A-Ride
   Seeds, Fertilizer & Cultivation Service
   Youth Community Conservation Improvement
   Self-Help and Resource Exchange
   Low-Income Fuel Assistance
   Man Power
   New Career
   Plan Assuring College Education (PACE)
   Senior Citizens Program
   Specialized Opportunity Services
   Emergency Fuel
   Volunteers In Service To America
   Rural Concentrated Employment Program
   Community Cannery
   Home Repair
   Volunteer Income Tax Assistance
   Summer Youth Recreation

Union County Community Action, 9 current programs
Wake County Opportunities, Inc., 13 current programs and spinoffs:
    Wake County Opportunities
    Housing Corporation
W.A.M.Y. Community Action, 9 current programs and spinoffs:
    Blue Ridge Heathside Crafts Cooperative
    Coordinated Human Services Transportation System
    Elderly Nutrition Program
    Green Eagle Rural Transportation Cooperative
    Head Start
Wayne Action Group for Economic Solvency, 9 current programs
Western Carolina Community Action, 14 current programs and spinoffs:
    Henderson County Council on Aging
    Helping Hand Day Care Center
    Human Resources Development Program
    Nurses Aide Training
    Mobile Rural Employment Service
    Play and Learn Day Care Center
Yadkin Valley Economic District, 22 current programs and
    spinoff:
Northwest Child Development Council

From *The Boston Globe*, July 24, 1997

The Media's Skewed Images

CHICAGO. The poet Langston Hughes once said the white music industry had "taken my blues and gone." He said the industry "fixed 'em so they don't sound like me." He would appreciate how the media covers poverty.

White Americans make up 67 percent of the nation's poor. But it is African-Americans who make up 65 percent of the images of poverty on the major television networks and 62 percent of the poor photographed in major news magazines, according to a recent study by Yale University political scientist Martin Gilens.

The stereotyping, discussed here last week at the National Association of Black Journalists convention, is a huge reason why the poor are being flogged. New laws have erased 3.1 million people from welfare rolls since 1993, though many states, including Massachusetts, have no clue if the majority of ex-recipients have jobs that pay above the poverty line.

Welfare was never popular, but Gilens said that "the racial component has added significant anger with it. . . . The effect is very direct. The greater the misrepresentation of black people receiving welfare, the more opposition whites have of welfare."

Gilens reviewed 635 photographs and images of poor people in *Newsweek, Time* and *US News and World Report*, and 1,100 like images from ABC, NBC, and CBS TV broadcasts from 1988 to 1992. Though census data shows that 51 percent of the poor actually work, news magazines fuel stereotypes of them as lazy.

Only 15 percent of the poor in magazines were working poor. While 42 percent of African-Americans in poverty have work, only 12 percent of poor African-Americans in the magazines had a job.

When photos were grouped by topic, black images dominated issues that evoke little political sympathy. African-Americans are 27 percent of the poor, but were 100 percent of people in pieces on the "underclass." African-Americans were 57-69 percent of the subjects of stories on housing, education, and money for the poor.

African-American images fell below 50 percent on topics that have public support. African-Americans were 40 percent of people in articles on employment programs and only 17 percent of those in stories on Medicaid. The media focus on out-of-wedlock children and lazy fathers erased the elderly black poor. Though 88 percent of poor African-Americans are over 64, only 1 percent of African-Americans in media poverty are over 64.

The media images have so brainwashed America that Gilens wrote that "personal experience appears to have little impact on public perceptions of the racial composition of poverty." Americans believe that African-Americans make up 47-50 percent of the nation's poor. That figure does not change whether a person is in Michigan or Pennsylvania where African-Americans make up 31 percent of the poor, or in North Dakota or Wyoming, where African-Americans are only 1 percent of the poor.

The brainwashing is impervious to education. In a 1994 New York Times/CBS poll, 47 percent of high school dropouts, 59 percent of high school graduates, and 48 percent of college grads said that most poor people were black. African-Americans are as prone as white Americans to say most of the poor are black.

As a part of his study, Gilens asked photo editors at the three magazines why they gave poverty such a black face. The most popular excuse is that the offices of magazines are in cities making the urban poor a close target of photographers' lenses.

To be sure, there are many extreme-poverty census tracts in which African-Americans are more than 60 percent of the poor, but overall, even in the nation's 10 largest metropolitan areas, African-American poverty is 32 percent, not a happy thought, but far under the 65 percent and 62 percent depictions in TV and magazines.

Gilens said that the photo editors guessed, on average, that 42 percent of the poor were black. Gilens said one editor said that some "subtle racism" may drive photo selection. The results of the racism are not subtle. Gilens cited a survey that found that when a white person was the subject of a story on unemployment, 71 percent of white viewers said unemployment was among the nation's three top problems. The percentage dropped to 53 percent when the story was about jobless African-Americans.

"Furthermore," Gilens wrote, "public support for efforts to redress racial inequality is likely to be diminished by the portrait of poverty found in these news magazines." In music, America took the black blues and fixed it so white singers would make the money. On poverty, the media beats the truth so black and blue, it helps guarantee that money for education and jobs do not go to anyone poor. They've taken the blues and gone. This time, a lot of people left voiceless were white.

Derrick Z. Jackson is a *Globe* columnist. (c) 1997, used by permission, *THE BOSTON GLOBE*.

From *The War Against The Poor,* by Herbert J. Gans

Selections from pages 90 to 101

The Uses of Undeservingness

Page 90

It is even possible to guess that the final bottom line or sufficient cause of the undeservingness of the poor is not their threats, actual or imaginary, to the mainstream population. Instead, what may energize feelings of undeservingness above all is the perceived insolence of the poor in behaving as they do while being supported by public funds.

Page 92

Two Microsocial Functions
RISK REDUCTION. . . Perhaps the primary use of the idea of the undeserving poor---primary because it takes place on the microsocial scale of everyday life---is that it distances the labeled from those who label them.
SUPPLYING OBJECTS OF REVENGE AND REPULSION. . . They can become such objects because their undeservingness justifies feelings of superiority on the part of the better-off classes.

Page 93

Three Economic Functions
CREATING JOBS FOR THE BETTER-OFF POPULATION. . . The larger the number of people who are declared undeserving, the larger also the number of people needed to modify, police, control, or guard them. These include the police, judges, lawyers, court probation officers, guards, and others who staff the criminal courts and prisons, as well as the social workers, psychiatrists, doctors, and others, and their support staffs, in "special" schools, drug treatment centers, homeless

shelters, mental hospitals, and the like.

SUPPLYING ILLEGAL GOODS. . . . Parts of the informal economy that make or sell legal goods or supply legal services but do so under illegal conditions may also attract the undeserving poor, such as welfare recipients or ex-convicts.

STAFFING THE RESERVE ARMY OF LABOR. . . Traditionally, the poor, including even the deserving ones, served the function of staffing the "reserve army of labor." As such they were available to be hired as strikebreakers, they were also invisible presences who could be used to break unions, harass unionized workers, or just scare them into working for less, and thus drive down wage rates.

Page 95

Three Normative Functions

MORAL LEGITIMATION. . . As a result, all institutions and social structures that stigmatize and exclude the undeserving concurrently offer moral and political legitimacy to the institutions and structures of the deserving.

VALUE REINFORCEMENT. . . When the undeserving poor violate, or are imagined to be violating, mainstream behavioral patterns and values, they help to reinforce and reaffirm the desirability of these patterns and values.

Page 97

POPULAR CULTURE VILLAINS. . . The undeserving poor have also played a continual role in supplying America with popular culture villains. . . The primary role of these villains is value-reinforcing, showing that crime and other norm violations do not pay.

Page 98

Three Political Functions

68

INSTITUTIONAL SCAPEGOATING. . . Institutional scapegoating takes some or all of the responsibility off the shoulders of elected and appointed officials who are supposed to deal with these problems.

Page 99

CONSERVATIVE POWER SHIFTING. . . Due partly to its ability to ignore the stigmatized poor, the political system can pay greater attention to the white-collar and professional classes.

SPATIAL STIGMATIZATION. . . Poor areas can be stigmatized as "underclass areas," making them eligible for other uses.

Page 100

Two Macrosocial Functions

REPRODUCTION OF STIGMA AND THE STIGMATIZED. . . For centuries now, undeservingness has enabled agencies that are established for helping the poor to evade their responsibilities. Indeed, these agencies, and the policies and programs they pursue, prevent many of the stigmatized from shedding their stigma, and also unwittingly manage to see to it that their children face the same hostility and thus grow up poor.

Page 101

FORCING THE POOR OUT OF THE LABOR FORCE. . . Ultimately, perhaps the most important function of undeservingness is to push the poor completely out of the labor force. People who have been labeled as undeserving may first be banished from the formal labor market and forced into the informal economy and the criminal underworld. Banishing the undeserving poor from that labor market can also be used to reduce the official jobless rate, a useful political function for election campaign purposes.

Published by Basic Books, 1995. Used by permission of Professor Gans.

Chapter 6

EDUCATORS

Poverty is ingrained in our total culture and involves all of our educational, economic, governmental, and religious institutions. Their structures and practices perpetuate poverty. Nevertheless, these institutions provide the means by which systemic poverty can be overcome. In the embrace of our culture these institutions are interrelated, but because each has a distinctive social role they need to be examined one by one. As we do so our attention moves from what poverty does to the poor to what poverty does to us, the non-poor.

While most people know that poverty is a blight, they do not realize thatdeprivation, isolation, hostility, and loss of talent which characterize poverty threaten the nation's social fabric, and are a time bomb already leaking corrosive acids into the whole society. Because poverty is frequently met by indifference, accepting things as they are, and denigrating those on whom we depend, it is clear that most do not know how our system functions in relation to those at the bottom. They do not know because it has never been part of their education.

Present attitudes and limited knowledge are barriers to under-standing poverty's threat to all of us. And the most serious barrier is the common assumption that the causes of poverty are the inadequacies of poor people. Most people have never had an opportunity to learn that poverty is also caused by the arranged structures of our social system. So for most of us the barrier is simply ignorance.

For this reason overcoming poverty must begin with helping the non-poor understand the realities of a system which depends on poverty. That is an educational task.

"Education" can connote a wide range of activities and organizations, formal and non-formal, all of which participate in shaping the public's ideas and practices. Those who assume that poverty is caused by the inadequacies of the poor naturally believe that the best way for us to combat poverty is to begin through education of the young. These people charge that public schools must prepare children and young people for jobs and adult responsibilities. These are valuable social contributions but they miss the more basic issue.

The thinking, beliefs, and commitments of children and young people (as well as of their parents) are probably more deeply influenced by other educating agencies: advertising, friends, church, television, newspapers, and books. Most non-formal educating agencies mix information with persuasion to promote common cultural values. At present these other educating channels perpetuate the assumption that the poor are to blame for their condition.

Educators of both leaders and the public at large need to make vivid what we have just reviewed. Poverty is perpetuated by stereotypes which misrepresent reality, by the historic dependence of our society on the employed poor built into inherited institutional structures, by the failure of those in power to recognize the true dimensions of poverty's long-term blight, by the many ways in which the poverty sector benefits the non-poor, and by the need of those in power to maintain the political, religious, economic, and cultural character of our society.

It is unfair to expect public schools, or the public media, to educate us about the complex poverty situation and also, at the same time, to open the door to more appropriate ways for dealing with it. The expectation is unfair because those who teach teachers have failed in their task.

Teachers and other leaders in the field of education are prepared by universities. This means that a basic responsibility of universities is to help leaders and the public at large understand the poverty system. Their task needs to be done before poverty can be addressed realistically.

Universities

The willingness of a university to accept such an assignment depends on how it views its social role. Universities, through scholarship and libraries, preserve our heritage. With that heritage as a base they prepare each generation of leaders for their tasks.

If universities are to prepare their graduates to face the realities of poverty they must confront their powerful historic institutional traditions. For universities, as for churches, addressing the present always involves dealing with the past. Our patterns of business and government are products of only three or four centuries; the roots of universities reach back at least to the eighth century, and of churches a thousand years more.

We all know that some professionals, such as doctors, lawyers, architects, and teachers, must have university preparation in order to practice their professions, and becoming employed in many other fields requires having a college or university degree. But the special role of the university is the preparation of those who are to provide those university courses, that is, the university as a teacher of teachers, the top level of educational impact upon a society.

We all know that universities are sponsored and supported in various ways, some by private organizations such as churches or industries, and others by governments, whether city, state, or national.

We also know there are state and national organizations which exert control of administration practice as well as curricular standards in the preparation of those teachers of teachers.

We all know that university studies are divided by departments and schools and that separate institutes or programs have been established in universities to carry on research.

We know, too, that universities occupy special space, most with a campus, where separate buildings are provided for classrooms, administration, housing and feeding, recreation, medical services, large group and small group activities.

We also know that universities vary both in levels of control by administration, faculty and students, as well as in teaching methods and equipment.

What most of us may never have had an opportunity to learn is how these structures and practices developed, and how they have become accepted as normal in our society.

72

You can check out the aspects noted above in your local university, or you can make each the subject of extensive study. Our objective here is to point to illustrations of some of these as an invitation for further exploration and reflection about how universities can help future leaders understand the way society deals with poverty as well as examine their capacity for leading in new directions for action.

When we embark on such an exploration we are immediately aware that the structures and patterns reviewed above did not happen by chance but developed in different times, under different pressures, in different places, and by different means.

Examining the character and function of universities is crucial to understanding the way a society deals with poverty, and doubly important in exploring how the devastation of poverty can be overcome. Awareness of this rootage helps us understand why universities are often very conservative in structure and practices. Although there have been great changes over the centuries, as Clark Kerr points out in the For Reflection section of this chapter, it is helpful to briefly review the long history of universities in Western cultures, and in doing so to identify some of the deposits of their history.

In Bologna, Italy, in the eighth century some students formed an association that set a pattern for similar groups in other cities. This type of association for study was later called a *studium generale* and it spread to cities all over the continent. In Bologna students adopted the curriculum, chose the teachers, and controlled the process, such as rules which imposed fines on teachers for being late to class. Bologna was primarily a law school and one of its distinctive contributions was teaching by the case method. While present students do not have the level of control students exercised in Bologna, the choices of students often has significant impact on courses offered and facilities provided, and therefore of positions professors may hold. The case method is still employed in many university fields.

By the twelfth century the term "university" applied to various kinds of associations. According to historian Hastings Rashdall the term was particularized as "University of Scholars," or "University of Study," or "University of Scholars and Masters." "There were, however, at the beginning of the thirteenth century three *studia* to which the term was pre-eminently applied and which enjoyed a unique and transcendent prestige: they were Paris for theology and arts, Bologna for law, and Salerno for medicine."[8]

According to Rashdall, the term *studium generale* implied, "1) that the school attracted or at least invited students from all parts, not merely those of a particular country or district; 2) that it was a place of higher education, that one of the higher faculties—theology, law, medicine— was taught there; 3) that such subjects were taught by a considerable number, or at least by a plurality, of masters."[9] "The process of welding the faculties into the university system was completed in 1281, when a university statute formally laid down (by the Pope) the principle that the acts of the faculty are the acts of the university."[10] And, "In the latter part of the fifteenth century the whole energy of the university was absorbed in constant conflicts with all manner of civil and ecclesiastical authorities on questions of privilege."[11]

Early universities are further described in the "For Reflection" section of this chapter. Universities sought independence from restrictions of local political and religious powers, and often obtained certain liberties by appealing to Rome for a charter. In the long run that led to other limitations on their freedom. By 1520, all universities in Europe were Roman Catholic. Several had student bodies in the thousands. While there was a close relation between church and university, there was also continuing tension. Such centralized control is now exercised through standards set by national associations.

Some historians of the period hold that generally the university course of study was meager, fixed and formal; that it leaned toward dogmatism and disputation; and dealt entirely with books. Yet historians also recognize that those same universities contributed to intellectual development and nurtured such minds as those of Dante, Petrarch, Boccaccio, and Erasmus in the field of literature; Wyclif, Hus, and Luther in the fields of theology and ecclesiastics.

Fundamental changes came when the Renaissance and the Reformation broke apart the Roman system and universities began the slow process of developing ways to maintain internal power over such matters as curriculum, setting standards, and giving degrees. In the process they developed ways to defend their independence from control by church or king.

Issues of authority, faculty responsibility, separation of disciplines, and outside pressures for control, have commanded the attention of universities again and again. Since institutions of higher education have been influenced by different historical events and the cultural character of their countries, many of those developments contribute to their highly varied patterns and struggles.

Even greater changes emerged in modern universities and are illustrated by differing concepts of their function in society. *The Concept of A University*, by Kenneth R. Minogue, presents strong support of academics. Jaroslav Pelikan's "Reexamination" of John Henry Cardinal Newman's *The Idea of the University* emphasizes the liberal arts and "Christian humanism". And the need for universities to focus on the problem of dealing with outside pressures is obvious in Alexander M. Mood's, *The Future of Higher Education*, in the Carnegie Foundation continuing series on Higher Education, and suggests that returning preparation of professionals to internships, following probably a year of general studies in the classroom, might be the wave of the future.

Traditions from that long history can be both aids and barriers to the task of educating society. Getting universities to introduce the study of poverty as a new academic field is a daunting task. But while traditions shape the way institutions of higher education function, Clark Kerr and the other writers show that the tradition itself is constantly being reshaped. Of particular interest is the long delay, following the industrial revolution when modern patterns of poverty developed, in universities establishing programs of study to address this social issue. Most colleges and universities assume that problems of poverty are addressed by sociologists and social workers, but departments or schools devoted to such study arrived on the scene in the late 19th and early 20th centuries. Many universities still leave the study of poverty to sociology and social work, and often professors challenge each other by their commitment to one or another theory about the poor. And the dominant approach has continued the assumptions of prior centuries that the proper way to deal with poverty is to provide services for the poor. A vivid example is spelled out in a book on social work treatment which lists 22 theories noted in the For Reflection section of this chapter.

How a university is related to poverty may be influenced by its sponsorship and control, location, mission statement, nature of the administration, political structure, character of the student body, basic curricula, professional schools and institutes, investment policies, and employment practices.

Three of these influences have direct implications for our concern: the nature of the student body, the curricula of professional schools, and the universities' employment practices for those at the bottom.

Campus Community

Faculty and students share a world of intellectual challenge, of leisure to reflect on knowledge gained from teaching or research, of escape (by some students) from the practical demands of making a living, and of comradery with others who look forward to being leaders in the world. While they are at the university, faculty and students are mostly protected from encounter with the world of the poor.

On the graduate level, the population of the university world includes those served by, or participating in, numerous research institutes, and those who use its libraries or buy its books. Faculty members participate in various professional associations which are elaborately developed (the bylaws of the American Educational Studies Association require 26 pages), by which they acquire status and advancement in the field. For faculty the university is also as elaborate as any other bureaucratic corporation. Lionel S. Lewis describes this in great detail in *Scaling the Ivory Tower*.[12]

In addition, alumni are the focus of support, but sometimes are a pressure for change. Many universities, like other institutions, generate powerful patterns that resist any challenge to their privileges, ambitions, opportunities, and concerns. All of this leaves little time or space for concerns about the poor, and it poses the question, on what grounds can one appeal to universities to add that concern? One form of resistance to change arises from the obvious fact that most universities are communities of the non-poor. The world of the ivory tower is about as far as you can get from the world of the ghetto.

Curriculum

Mission statements make it obvious that the focus of university commitment is to contribute to the success of those at, or seeking to rise to, the top in their chosen fields.

One university emphasizes "original inquiry" while another stimulates "intellectual growth" and still another explains its task as "encouraging habits of mind that ask why?" Such foci may provide hints of studies that could include people at the bottom, but we cannot be sure. Such statements can be read to suggest that the requisite "knowledge" is already in hand or is being researched, and is being presented to students to do with as they choose.

A quite different mission would focus on being inquisitive, exploratory, and on seeking and discovering new perspectives on significant realities in the world around them. Or of seeing civic responsibility as a necessary use of academic achievement.

It is possible that professors of history, psychology, religion, economics, literature, as well as sociology, occasionally include information and insights into that "other world," but course descriptions in university catalogues rarely include any explicit study of "poverty."

The national Rural Sociological Society set up a special task force on rural poverty courses, which reported in 1993, "When the Task Force on Persistent Rural Poverty accepted the challenge of increasing the attention paid to rural poverty in college and university curricula, we had no idea how great the challenge would be. We were able (in two years) to identify only a dozen or so courses being taught in the United States today which address the problem of rural poverty."[13] Many of the issues raised in the courses reviewed apply to urban poverty as well.

An inevitable barrier is that curricular change usually means that existing courses must be dropped to make room for new courses. The process of considering a new course can involve several levels of faculty and administrative approval. When no professor is prepared to offer such a course or press for its inclusion, the possibilities of such a step are sharply limited.

Another handicap in attempting to introduce a poverty course is the lack of student interest, desire, or pressure for such study. It is women in the student body who press for women's studies, and African American students who press for African American study programs; but in an academic community of the non-poor there is little incentive on the part of students to try to understand the subject.

Usually the subject of poverty is considered a concern of just one discipline, sociology, but that field has analyzed social structures and functions primarily by class analysis. The principal problem arising from that limited approach is its failure to distinguish among the poor between those who do not "work" and those who do, and among those who do work, the distinction between those who work on their own and those who are employed. This is a crucial matter and is the primary reason almost no attention is given, even in this field, to the significance of millions of people who are employed in essential jobs and still are poor.

Professional Preparation

From the medieval period to the present a distinctive feature of a university has been its professional schools. Today universities prepare graduates who inevitably will deal with the poor and poverty issues in their professional practices: doctors, clergy, nurses, sociologists, lawyers, bankers, editors, newscasters, economists, teachers, city managers, legislators, public administrators, business managers, and social workers. The absence of the study of poverty from their professional preparation is one reason why we all share in perpetuating injustice toward the poor.

There are differences in the way such professionals encounter the poor, and in the factors that have to be taken into account as they make professional decisions. Eventually there may be good reasons to develop advanced studies specific to a profession, as well as broader studies of the relation of poverty to crime, environment, gender, race, and to power, but the present need is for an introduction to the field of poverty studies that includes insights from many disciplines.

Specific handicaps face universities in any attempt to overcome their sins of omission: the intra-university time-consuming and political process of curricular change; the reality that there may be no professor who has either taken or taught such a course; and the lack of concern among professional associations and alumni that might urge such a brave step.

Employer

Another significant way a university is involved with poverty is its wage schedule for workers. University staff members who provide nonprofessional, yet essential, services sometimes earn less than employees at grocery stores, professional offices, and industries down the street. These essential workers prepare and serve meals, clean rooms, mow the lawn, wash windows, and provide secretarial services for faculty.

A preliminary glance shows that the problem of pay for maintenance, clerical, food services, and dining facilities employees has been a troubling issue for many universities across the country. A news item from *The Chronicle of Higher Education* recounts Yale University's explanation for its decision to wait a year before settling with its 3,700 striking workers. The account is included in the For Reflection section of this chapter. The university as an employer is confronted by the same pressures and opportunities as employers in other sectors.

* * * * *

FOR REFLECTION

From *The Reformation in Education*, by Eugene Magevney, S.J.

Page 16

At the time of Luther's secession, in 1520, there were in Europe 72 universities, all of them Catholic, of course . . .

Page 30

The ancient University of Prague, so celebrated in its day, and which, at the beginning of the fifteenth century could boast of 60,000 students, had in 1550 dwindled to eight professors and 30 pupils. That of Vienna, which in 1519 matriculated 661 studentsw, in 1532 received only 12. That of Cologne, where 2,000 students had been the regular attendance from 1500 to 1510, in 1534 had 54. The University of Erfurt, Luther's Alma Mater, and where we might easily presume, the light of his educational reform shone brightest, had in 1521 only 311 pupils, and in 1527 sank to 14. Freiburg in 1617 had 78 pupils. The professors of the University of Heidelberg were forced to resign their chairs and seek a livelihood in some other direction.

Published by The Cathedral Library Association of New York, 1903.

———

From *The Universities of Europe in the Middle Ages*, by Hastings Rashdall

Page 137

In the eleventh and twelfth century, religion exercised at least as powerful an influence upon human affairs in Italy as it did in the north of Europe; but here even religious questions assumed a political shape. Bologna was absorbed with the questions about Investiture, about the relation of Papacy and Empire, Church and State, feudalism and civic liberty, while the schools of France were distracted by questions about the unity of intellect, about transubstantiation, about the reality of universals.

Page 151

The student-universities represented an attempt on the part of such men (young men of good position in their own cities) to create for themselves an artificial citizenship in place of the natural citizenship which they had temporarily renounced in the pursuit of knowledge or advancement; and the great importance of a studium to the commercial welfare of the city in which it was situated may explain the ultimate willingness of the municipalities, though the concession was not made without a struggle, to recognize these student-communities.
Published by the Oxford University Press, 1895.

From *The German Universities and University Study*, by Friedrich Paulsen

Page 16

Unlike the first French and Italian institutions, the German universities did not originate spontaneously, but were the result of a definite scheme in which, as a rule, the civil and ecclesiastical authorities were both interested. The actual founders were the territorial governments, or perhaps the municipalities. The ruler called the school into being, supplied it with buildings and endowments, and, at the same time, granted the *universitas* certain corporate rights, such as autonomy, jurisdiction over its own members, and exemption from duties and taxes. The next step was to secure recognition from the higher authorities, especially the papal, from whom was procured, for a price, a "bull" which finally sanctioned the establishment and endowment of the university and authorized it to teach, hold examinations, and confer degrees. In this latter arrangement we see clearly the medieval notion of instruction as an ecclesiastical function. Somewhat later it became customary to procure the imperial sanction as well, for the imperial power also had something of the glamour of universality about it, and besides, the view had become prevalent that the Roman law was also the

"imperial" law. Freiburg began this practice. The new university thus became a *studium privilegiatum* or "privileged school."
Published by Charles Scribner's Sons, 1906.

From *A History of the University of Oxford*, by G.C. Broderick

Page 69

The great educational movement which sprang from the Reformation was essentially popular rather than academical, and by no means tended to increase the relative importance of the Universities.

Page 92

"Thenceforth (1629) the University of Oxford once open to all Christendom, was narrowed into an exclusively Church of England institution, and became the favorite arena of Anglican controversy, developing more and more that special charter, at once worldly and clerical, which it shares with Cambridge among the Universities of Europe.
Published by Anson D.F. Randolph & Co., New York, no date.

From *The Story of the University of Edinburgh During Its First Three Hundred Years*, by Sir Alexander Grant (1884)

Page 126

The King was not to found a University, but was to give full powers to the Town Council, with the advice of the Ministers, to found a College or Colleges, for the higher studies. And the municipal authorities and clergy of Edinburgh were entrusted forever with the absolute control of higher education within the burgh. . . The precedent and the model in this matter was Geneva, to which the Scottish Kirk looked as the fountain-head of its doctrine and discipline, Geneva which had been the asylum for refugee Scottish Reformers from 1554 to 1560. In the republic of Geneva the Municipal Council was of course supreme; and in 1559, while the place was still full of Scotchmen, that Council had, by the advice of Calvin, opened their Academy. The Academy failed, as we have seen, to obtain recognition as a University from the King of France. But it at once rose to be a distinguished seat of learning.

Published by Longmans, Green and Co., London, 1884.

From *The Uses of the University*, by Clark Kerr

Pages 1, 2

The Idea of a Multiversity

The university started as a single community, a community of masters and students. It may even be said to have had a soul in the sense of a central animating principle. Today the large American university is, rather, a whole series of communities and activities held together by a common name, a common governing board, and related purposes. This great transformation is regretted by some, accepted by many, gloried in, as yet, by few. But it should be understood by all.

The university of today can perhaps be understood, in part, by comparing it with what it once was, with the academic cloister of Cardinal Newman, with the research organism of Abraham Flexner. Those are the ideal types from which it has derived, ideal types which still continue the illusions of some of its inhabitants. The modern American university, however, is not Oxford nor is it Berlin; it is a new type of institution in the world. As a new type of institution, it is not really private and it is not really public; it is neither entirely of the world nor entirely apart from it. It is unique.

"The Idea of a University" was, perhaps, never so well expressed as by Cardinal Newman when engaged in founding the University of Dublin a little over a century ago. His views reflected the Oxford of his day whence he had come. A university, wrote Cardinal Newman, is "the high protecting power of all knowledge and science, of fact and principle, of inquiry and discovery, of experiment and speculation; it maps out the territory of the intellect, and sees that . . . there is neither encroachment nor surrender seen on any side." He favored "liberal knowledge," and said that "useful knowledge" was a "deal of trash."

Page 4

"The Idea of a Modern University," to use Flexner's phrase, was already being born. "A University," said Flexner in 1930, "is not outside, but inside the general social fabric of a given era. It is not something apart, something historic, something that yields as little as possible to forces and influences that are more or less new. It is on the contrary . . . an expression of the age, as well as an influence operating upon both present and future."

Page 6

By 1930, American universities had moved a long way from Flexner's "Modern University" where "The heart of a university is a graduate school of arts and science, the solidly professional schools (mainly, in America, medicine and law) and certain research institutes." They were becoming less and less like a "genuine university," by which Flexner meant "an organism, characterized by highness and definiteness of aim, unity of spirit and purpose." The "Modern University" was as nearly dead in 1930 when Flexner wrote about it, as the Old Oxford was in 1852 when Newman idealized it. History moves faster than the observer's pen. Neither the ancient classics and theology nor the German philosophers and scientists could set the tone for the really modern university, the multiversity.

Pages 17, 18

Out of all these fragments, experiments, and conflicts a kind of unlikely consensus has been reached. Undergraduate life seeks to follow the British, who have done the best with it, and an historical line that goes back to Plato; the humanists often find their sympathies here. Graduate life and research follow the Germans, who once did best with them, and an historical line that goes back to Pythagoras; the scientists lend their support to all this. The "lesser" professions (lesser than law and medicine) and the service activities follow the American pattern, since the Americans have been best at them, and an historical line that goes back to the Sophists; the social scientists are more likely to be sympathetic. . . The resulting combination does not seem plausible but it has given America a remarkably effective educational institution. A university anywhere can aim no higher than to be as British as possible for the sake of the undergraduates, as German as possible for the sake of the graduates and the research personnel, as American as possible for the sake of the public at large, and as confused as possible for the sake of the preservation of the whole uneasy balance.

Pages 18, 19

The Governance of the Multiversity

The multiversity is an inconsistent institution. It is not one community but several: the community of the undergraduate and the community of the graduate; the community of the humanist; the community of the social scientist; and the community of the scientist; the community of the professional schools; the community of all the nonacademic personnel; the community of the administrators. Its edges are fuzzy; it reaches out to alumni, legislators, farmers, businessmen, who are all related to one or more of these internal communities. As an institution, it looks far into the past and far into the future, and is often at odds with the present. It serves society almost slavishly, a society it also criticizes, sometime unmercifully. Devoted to equality of opportunity, it is itself a class society. A community, like the medieval communities of masters and students, should have common interests in the multiversity, they are quite varied, even conflicting. A community should have a soul, a single animating principle; the multiversity has several, some of them quite good, although there is much debate on which souls really deserve salvation.

The multiversity is a name. This means a great deal more than it sounds as though it might. The name of the institution stands for a certain standard of performance, a certain degree of respect, a certain historical legacy, a characteristic quality of spirit. This is of the utmost importance to faculty and to students, to the government agencies and the industries with which the institution deals.

Page 28

The general rule is that the administration everywhere becomes, by force of circumstances if not by choice, a more prominent feature of the university. As the institution becomes larger, administration becomes more formalized and separated as a distinct function; as the institution becomes more complex, the role of administration becomes more central in integrating it; as it becomes more related to the once external world, the administration assumes the burdens of these relationships.

In his book, *Social Work Treatment, Interlocking Theoretical Approaches*, Francis J. Turner describes 22 theories, devoting a chapter to each:

Psychoanalytic Theory	The Problem-Solving Model
Functional Theory for Social Work Practice	Task-Centered Social Work
	Crisis Theory
Gestalt Theory	Neurolinguistic Programming Model
Cognitive Theory	Ego Psychology
Behavior Therapy	Client-Centered Theory
Meditation	Family Treatment
Existential Social Work	Transactional Analysis: A Social Work Treatment Model
Communication Theory	

Psychosocial Theory	Feminism and Social Work Practice
Systems Theory	Marxist Theory
Role Theory	The Life Model Approach to Social Work Practice

Yale and Its Union Workers Compromise to Resolve Labor Dispute

BY AMY MAGARO RUBIN

A bitter and very public labor dispute at Yale University has been resolved, with both sides gaining some of what they wanted.

The Federation of University Employees, which represents 3,700 workers at Yale, reached agreements with the university last month. One chapter of the union represents clerical workers; another represents dining hall and maintenance workers. They have separate contracts but shared many concerns during the dispute.

The new contracts give the workers annual raises ranging from 2 per cent to nearly 5 per cent over the next six years, along with a 10-year job guarantee. The contracts also allow Yale to use subcontractors for some service work.

Yale's desire to subcontract jobs currently performed by union workers was the key dispute in negotiations. The university saw the idea as a way to keep costs down.

"To retain our position as one of the world's great universities, we must have the flexibility to manage Yale efficiently and deliver high-quality services at a reasonable cost," Yale President Richard C. Levin said in October in a letter to Yale faculty and staff members and students.

Union officials objected to the plan, saying that many union members would be replaced with outside workers and that job quality and pay would diminish for those who remained. "Yale is the only source of decent-paying jobs in New Haven," said Deborah R. Chernoff, chief spokeswoman for the union. "Yale's plan would have a very depressive economic and social impact here."

THE RIGHT TO SUBCONTRACT

Under the six-year contracts, the union agreed to allow Yale to subcontract some work. In return, the university said that outside workers would be paid at least $7 an hour and that no union employees would lose their jobs or be given reduced hours because of subcontracting.

The union also acceded to Yale's plan to open four fast-food restaurants to supplement the campus dining halls, as long as they are staffed by union employees. Yale wants to bring in such franchises to give students more dining choices, but the union was opposed because it feared that the new jobs would be low-paying.

Officials on both sides called the new contracts a compromise, and the union declared them a victory for job security. "Every contract has compromise in it," said Ms. Chernoff, "but this is an unprecedented level of job security in this day and age." She added that she hoped the contracts would set a precedent for service employees at other colleges.

"When the university began its proposals, many people were saying that everybody is losing jobs, and that's just the way things are," she said. "This contract shows that you can successfully resist those attempts, and we hope that other employers take note."

Dr. Levin said in a statement that the contracts "provide Yale the flexibility it needs to manage its service and maintenance work more effectively." He also said he hoped that the agreements would lay the foundation for better relations between the union and the university.

TWO STRIKES

The labor dispute began in November 1995, when the union's contracts expired. In the course of 13 months of negotiations, workers staged two strikes, which disrupted classes and at one point forced the university to shut down all but one of its 12 dining halls.

Demonstrations were also held, attracting nationwide attention. John Sweeney, head of the A.F.L.-C.I.O., joined a group of 1,500 people last

88

month to protest Yale's plans shortly before the resolution was reached. Mr. Sweeney and 310 other demonstrators were arrested for blocking an intersection.

Chapter 7

EMPLOYERS

In considering the economics of poverty we need to understand that the United States has developed a distinctive structure of systemic poverty. Its architects are the employers of the working poor.

Distinguishing between the "working poor" and the "employed poor" is important for it provides a clearer picture of the crucial issue with which we are concerned. That issue is the two-way dependency of the employer-employee relationship as an exercise of economic power.

One interpretation of the relationship is that taking a job and becoming an employee implies a mutual arrangement between the parties. This may have been the case when the medieval vassal signed a Vatican-approved contract to serve the lord of the manor in exchange for land and provisions. However, the more modern relationship is one-sided, expressed as "I am giving you a job." In reality the employees are the more generous givers because, since their wages are less than it costs them to live, they are giving their lives.

We have already looked at the social consequences of workers being poor. Now we need to turn our attention from workers to employers, to their differences, what they expect of employees, how wages are determined, and the larger social impacts of their decisions.

Many "employed poor" work for individuals as domestics, painters, gardeners, baby sitters, attendants, chauffeurs. Schedules may be irregular and personal relationships may be important, but the determination of wages depends mainly on the judgment of the employer.

Someone who hires a maid is not prone to claim that it is a virtue to increase the maid's salary so that she can pay for child care. Nor does the employer usually worry about the fact that the maid cannot be at home taking care of her own children, or that she misses meals with her family. The employer depends on the maid to clean the house, cook good meals, prepare for parties, and be ready to help with extra guests.

A similar pattern of dependence is essential in a day care center where the employed poor are alter-parents who provide care, safety, and assist in the physical and emotional development of others' children; or in a nursing home give comfort, convenience, and encouragement to the elderly ill. Paying low wages for such services is usually taken for granted.

Another level of employment for the poor is in large organizations where relatively few jobs are done by workers at the bottom, where monotonous and routine jobs have already been mechanized or robotized, and where the wages set by management (or by those at national or international headquarters) are related to pay scales of the much larger number of employees above them. In these organizations (except where workers are unionized) there is no one to press for wages that are fair to bottom workers, or to point out the social consequences of low pay. For these organizations the pay of those at the bottom has little to do with the "bottom line" because these essential workers receive such a small portion of the economy of the corporation.

Then there are organizations in which the great majority of workers receive low pay and a small number of managers direct what they do. Cut and sew operations, fast food chains, those who employ seasonal workers to pick fruit and dig vegetables, and many others are totally dependent on the poor they employ for their existence, their profits, and their power.

Corporate America comes in many patterns and the proportion of employed poor indicates the dimensions of dependence on those workers. Public attention may be focused on total sales, CEO salaries, and fluctuations in stock prices, but whatever may be happening to corporations at the top, it is the employed poor who provide the indispensable cushion on which they all rest.

We need not spell out all aspects of this dependence in corporate life, but food may be the most obvious, for no organization can do without it. Every item on the menu of organizations that provide meals is the end of a long chain of production and distribution.

One can start with A as for apples. At every step, from pruning the trees, through cultivating, picking, grading, selecting, packing, transporting, storing, displaying, buying, preparing and baking the pie a waitress brings to the table, the employed poor provide essential service. The same pattern applies to similar steps in the production of all foods from apricots to zucchini.

Even if they wanted to it would not be easy for corporations to explain their dependence on the poor for both production and services, nor would it be acceptable to describe the importance of the employed poor in advertisments or in impressive annual reports. Those omissions may be inadvertent, or thoughtless, or taken for granted, maybe for shame, but the consequence is a misrepresentation which prevents stockholders from knowing what keeps the corporation functional.

But workers are referred to when corporate employers report reductions in labor costs. So they are not really "The Forgotten Americans," a popular phrase during the Depression. They are listed when downsizing is reported. They are remembered for what they do without. What is recognized and applauded as an economic accomplishment is in fact a social disaster.

Corporate advertising wants people to buy its products or services even as the corporation denies their employees the ability to do so. This was Henry Ford's defense for paying his workers a munificent $5.00 a day. "Otherwise, how can they buy cars?" he asked. In *A Living Wage*, Lawrence B. Glickman reviews in detail America's economic discussion about fair wages and points out the emphasis of many on the fact that workers are also consumers, not just producers.[14]

The environmental movement has frequently focused on "real cost," pointing out how such items as gasoline use results in public health expenditures that are far greater than the price at the pump. What is the "real cost" to society of having one-third of the children in the country live in poor housing, go to poor schools, and be subjected to the dangers of neglected neighborhoods? These are social impacts of every decision about low pay.

These examples illustrate the fact that the society has to pay the "real cost" one way or another. Decisions about wages are usually made with attention to the economic welfare of the institution, not in terms of their possible long-range effects, either for the employees or for the society at large. Having given little attention to those consequences, employers have no means by which to measure them. As a result, they do not comprehend what the "real costs" are or how they could be calculated.

Employers bemoan the high costs of government programs that attempt to deal with those consequences but have little awareness of how their "cost reduction" requires increases in social costs. Most employers would find it very difficult to admit this as their responsibility. They are much more aware of the "bottom line" and expectations of stockholders that they increase profits, than they are of the damaging effect their low pay has on their workers.

Eliminating systemic poverty is primarily a private sector, rather than a government sector, responsibility. It raises many problems: the growing use of part-time or "temporary" workers; rapidly changing technology; the rise of new kinds of businesses; the increase of women in the workforce; and the possibilities of doing many jobs from the home. All of these complicate the relationship between employers and employees.

It is as though employers of all kinds are saying, "Society, it is your responsibility to prepare workers ready to do any kind of job we need done, wherever and whenever we need them, and at whatever level of pay we choose. You benevolent people should help provide low-paid workers with food, clothing, and shelter, and you charitable organizations should see that the workers are educated and healthy. For those of us in business, our responsibility is to manage the organization efficiently so that it provides profits for owners and stockholders."

Justifying Low Pay

The poverty of the employed poor is not caused by the inadequacies of individuals but by decisions of private sector employers. When employers are challenged, the common justification of low wages is "the market." They say "we pay what the market requires," and for some their opposition to a "minimum wage" is because they believe that the government is corrupting the operation of the "free market" system.

Arguments about "the market" are very much on the minds of leaders in countries now shifting to "free enterprise" systems. Adam Smith is credited with introducing the idea of the market as the arbiter of wages. In *The Wealth of Nations* he described the natural "propensity of human nature" to barter and exchange one thing for another. The value of these exchanges, Smith argued, was "led by an invisible hand." The For Reflection section of this chapter offers various interpretations of Smith's views.

The dramatic metaphor of an invisible hand directing the value of labor was ardently welcomed by those who set wages: managers, owners, corporations, boards of trustees, investors, etc. It freed them from any moral responsibility for the results of low wages. The mechanisms of "the market" were and are the working of competition (the availability of many low-skilled people prevents workers from asking for more pay) and the operation of supply and demand for goods and services.

Some contend that competition is a social benefit. The authors of *Economics as Social Science* claim that "the economics profession in general is obsessed with a felt need to show that competition maximizes the general welfare."[15] And they quote William Baumol's declaration as president of the American Economic Association, that "In the received analysis perfect competition serves as the one standard of welfare-maximizing structure and behavior."[16]

A second reason offered to justify low pay for employees doing bottom jobs is that they are thought of as low-skill jobs. That may be true of some but not of all. To classify as low skill the job of child-care worker or teacher assistant or nursing home aid is irresponsible. There may be some people doing these jobs who are not very good at it, but the child, the pupil, and the elderly ill deserve the best possible care. Those doing these jobs may vary in levels of ability but "dumbing down" the value of the job to justify low pay is unfair.

Continued justification of low pay fails to admit that the employed poor are absolutely essential to nearly every organized activity of our society. We all have to eat and we all need to be clothed. Nike shoes are not the only item of clothing that is made by people whose wages are less than it costs them to live. Should not necessity be considered in setting wages?

A second omission is responsibility. A baby-sitter is responsible. The bathroom in a hospital cleaned by a low-paid person must be as sanitary as the operating room. Providing safe food involves responsibility. Watching a gauge may not take much skill but it can be a crucial responsibility. And should not responsibility be a factor in determining pay?

Then there is the justification that the low-status job and low pay are the first rung on the ladder by which, with energy and persistence, one can climb into well-paying jobs. Bradley Schiller, in *The Economics of Poverty and Discrimination*, after giving statistics about the income of the working poor, writes, "If there is any moral to be gained from the foregoing figures, perhaps it is this: a poor janitor who works hard stands a very good chance of becoming a hard-working poor janitor."[17]

Another justification is almost as common as the appeal to the market. It is the claim "I cannot afford to pay more." That statement means one thing to the manager of a business and quite another for the manager of a non-profit organization. The business manager who pays low wages, knowing that they are less than the employee's cost of living, expects that government welfare programs or private charity will keep the employee alive, healthy, and able to get to work. This expectation expresses two assumptions: a) that every entrepreneur has a right to a profit, and b) that society should subsidize businesses that are unable to profit otherwise.

"I cannot afford to pay more" may also be claimed by the president of a college or university, pastor of a church, head of a national professional association, director of a museum, manager of a golf club, superintendent of schools, or executive of a community service organization. But the claim may not be true; rather, in each case, pay reflects a value judgment which seldom takes into account what it means to live in the world of the poor.

These are all "non-profits" that may have funds from benevolence, membership dues, charity, tuition fees, or taxes, or a combination of such sources. And because these organizations are widespread in the society, those choices usually reflect the taken-for-granted views of the general culture.

Competition, as a major feature of "the market," can have quite different implications for those businesses that are engaged in international trade. The common device for meeting that competition is to "join 'em" and transfer as much as possible of production, including whole plants, to countries where the hourly pay is much lower than in the United States. The pressures on business stemming from "free trade" involve both the nature of products (Japanese vs. American automobiles and technology) and lower wages paid in other countries (clothing from China and tomatoes from Mexico). And a corporation with branches in many countries is involved with complex pay scales as well as with different social settings and assumptions about work. This can be used as an escape from any social responsibility.

"The market" is different for organizations that conduct activities only within the United States. The pay scale for waiters at Hardees or McDonalds, or for those who clean offices at night in the World Trade Center in New York, the Department of Agriculture in Washington, or the Getty Museum near Los Angeles faces no competition from other countries. The assumption is that there are always plenty of people with low skills to fill such positions.

Another common device for keeping wages low is "privatizing" by governmental units, or "contracting out" by corporations, to non-union operations so that the workers are no longer government or corporate employees.

But for an employer who would like to give better pay to those at the bottom, a valid question is "how should that pay be determined?" or "what level of pay is fair?" That question is really "what is the real cost of doing business?" And "what is the local or regional cost of living?" This difficulty was recognized when Congress asked the National Academy of Sciences to define "poverty." That assignment stemmed from the fact that the "poverty line" based on 1950s circumstances is obsolete and therefore inappropriate. The Academy identified child care for working mothers, medical care, and new tax laws that reduce the disposable income of workers as illustrations of items that now should be included in figuring a fair cost of living.

It became apparent immediately that these items are as variable across the country as was the "minimal diet" of the 1950s. Although one member of the Academy committee contended that there should be an "absolute standard" he was only implying that there was no problem to be resolved. But the problem continues as long as there is a "means test" to determine who should, or should not, receive welfare.

Reactions to the discovery of the wages that children in Thailand received for making Nike shoes, a high-priced item in this country, indicates that many people are sensitive to unfair treatment of the employed poor. This suggests that determining a "living wage" and then encouraging employers of all kinds to pay it to all workers, at the bottom as well as at the top, will succeed only with general public support. We need to recognize that better pay for those at the bottom will require, in the short run, higher costs for all of us.

Serious consideration of this matter is handicapped until some research agency attempts to find out what paying a living wage to the employed poor would do to the cost of living of the rest of us. Again and again the idea is met by "raising the pay would raise the cost of living for the poor, too, so they would gain nothing." Yes, but consider this. If a living wage would raise the income of bottom workers by 100 percent, they will then be able to absorb the 5-10 percent increase of costs to all of us. The response to this point is usually, "I never thought of that."

Equally needed is research about how higher pay for the employed poor would impact the local economy. If we compare what happens to the expendable income of a janitor with the expendable income of the CEO we could assume that local costs for food, clothing, etc. would be somewhat similar, although somewhat higher for the CEO, than for the janitor. But for the CEO those local expenditures would be a very small percentage of his total income. The rest would be invested, one way or another and "go to Wall Street." The increased income of the janitor, however, would all go to the local grocery and clothing stores, the gas station and the doctor, before going to the bank and from there to Wall

Street. The flow into the local economy would be direct and significant.

The other side of the equation is that a decent income for the employed poor would lead to a sharp reduction in expenditure for the county, state, and federal welfare programs. It would make possible a safer place for the poor to live, and begin to replace despair with hope. This in turn would reduce the present huge bureaucracies of public and private charity agencies, and reduce costs for food stamps, subsidized housing, and legal services. It would reduce the indignity of having someone else making life decisions for the workers.

I have contended here that systemic poverty is produced and perpetuated by our dependence on the employed poor. While the most direct advantage is to employers, all of us benefit from this dependence. This suggests that although there may be several options, most of us will probably try to continue the present system and preserve our advantages. The social costs of poverty are high but we and our neighbors will find ways to escape them. We can support the cutting of taxes that pay for welfare (of the poor, that is). We can escape to our gated communities safe from dangers of the violent. And we can leave it to the benevolent to take care of poverty's problems.

However, if those who ask "What should be done about systemic poverty?" are genuinely concerned, and intend to do what they can to change the way this society treats its employed poor, then careful consideration of the question is justified.

In 1993 a serious nationwide series of group discussions was sponsored by the National Issues Forums based on a book, *The Poverty Puzzle*.[18] In that book the poor were identified as those with incomes below the "poverty line" and four "choices" were proposed:
1. Welfare Trap: Perverse Incentives and Failed Policies
2. The Rights of the Poor: Mending the Safety Net
3. Behavior Modification: A New Compact with the Poor
4. Jobs Strategy: Moving Beyond Welfare

Emphasizing the fourth choice, the book asserts that "the plight of the working poor underlies the need for decisive public action," and contends that "America's strategy for fighting poverty must begin with a clear message: those who work will not be poor."[19] That was significant message but the document did not go on to explore what that message implied. Instead, the emphasis was upon the responsibility of government to guarantee jobs for everyone. Jobs for everyone who can work is a worthy goal, but the forum series failed to address the need implied in their own "message." If the *employed* poor receive sufficient income to maintain a decent level of living, the largest percentage of "the poor" would be removed from the welfare system.

While America has its own distinct structure of social deprivation, poverty is a world-wide blight. Whether countries attempting to shift to a free enterprise system may be any more successful than America in overcoming poverty is yet to be seen. Facing reality head-on is required: the challenge is human rights for all. In neither the United States nor in other countries will this be attained by transferring wealth, but by the much more mundane process of paying a living wage so that the economy serves those on whom we depend for the bottom as well as the top jobs.

Thirty-five years ago Michael Harrington, in his dramatic and forceful depiction of The Other America, decried the increasing gap between the poor and the affluent in America.[20]

Article after article appearing in current newspapers assure us that the appalling gap continues to widen.

* * * * *

FOR REFLECTION

From *The End of Work, The Decline of the Global Labor Force and the Dawn of the Post-Market Era,* by Jeremy Rifkin

Pages 177, 178

The Other America

Two very different Americas are emerging as we make the turn into the twenty-first century. The new high-technology revolution is likely to exacerbate the growing tensions between rich and poor and further divide the nation into two incompatible and increasingly warring camps. The signs of social disintegration are everywhere. Even conservative political pundits are beginning to sit up and take notice. Author and political analyst Kevin Phillips worries about the emergence of "dual economies" and points to states like Pennsylvania and North Carolina, where high-tech, post-service cities like Philadelphia and Durham are prospering in the new global economic web, while other areas of the states are losing steel mills and textile plants, forcing thousands of workers onto the relief rolls.

Paul Saffo echoes Phillips' concerns. He notes that in high-tech enclaves like Telluride, Colorado, "You've got people living in electronic cottages making New York-scale salaries, while right next door there's someone else who's a hamburger flipper at the local fast food joint and he's making a rural Colorado salary." Saffo says that when "you get the ultra wealthy and the ultra poor cheek to cheek . . it's absolute political dynamite . . . and could lead to a social revolution."

The 1993 Census Bureau report on poverty in America provided statistical evidence of the growing gap between rich and poor. According to the study, the number of Americans living in poverty in 1992 is greater than at any other time since 1962. In 1992, 36.9 million Americans were living in poverty, an increase of 1.2 million over 1991 and 5.4 million more than in 1989. More than 40 percent of the nation's poor are children. The poverty rate among African-Americans now exceeds 33 percent and for Hispanics, 29.3 percent. Nearly 11.6 percent of all white Americans live in poverty.

Despite the fact that more than 40 percent of the nation's poor worked during 1992, they were not able to make ends meet with low-paying, often part-time employment. Their paltry incomes had to be supplemented with government-assisted relief efforts, just to survive. In 1992 more than 1 in 10 Americans depended on food stamps, the largest percentage since the federal program was launched in 1962. Nine million people have joined the food stamp program in just the past four years, bringing the number of Americans on food stamp assistance to 27.

million. Some experts estimate that another 20 million are currently eligible for food stamps but have failed to apply. Many of the new recipients are working people whose depressed wages and part-time employment are inadequate to feed their families. Others are the recently unemployed, the victims of global competition, corporate restructuring, and technology displacement.

In addition to government food assistance programs, more than 50,000 private food banks, pantries, and soup kitchens are distributing food to the nation's hungry. In Chicago the Greater Chicago Food Repository distributed more than 22 million pounds of food in 1992, including 48,000 meals every single day of the year.

Many of the nation's hungry are older Americans. Upwards of a million senior citizens are undernourished, and reports indicate that more than 30 million older people are forced to regularly skip meals. Hunger strikes most often among the nation's youth. One child in four growing up in the United States goes hungry, according to studies prepared by Bread for the World, a Washington-based relief organization. Don Reeves, an economic policy analyst for Bread for the World, says that the globalization of the economy and rapid technology displacement are "principal factors" in the growing numbers of American families who are going hungry.

Chronic hunger is a major contributing factor to escalating health-care costs. Low birth-weight infants and malnourished children often grow up with serious long-term health problems, adding billions of dollars to the health care bill. Many of the nation's poorest citizens have little or no access to adequate health care. According to the 1992 census, 28.5 percent of the poor have no health insurance of any kind.

Pages 179, 180

The nation's poor are concentrated in rural areas and in inner-city cores, the two regions hardest hit by technology displacement over the past two decades. More than 42 percent of the country's poor live in inner cities, up from 30 percent in 1968. The costs to society of "providing" for the nation's urban underclass now exceeds $230 billion a year, a staggering figure especially at a time when the nation is concerned about mounting debt and increased federal deficits.

A growing number of industry analysts fix the blame for the escalating poverty on intense global competition and changes in technology. Light manufacturing industries employing urban workers cut employment by upward of 25 percent or more in recent years. The editors of *Business Week* note that, "For urban workers who counted on steady factory jobs that required little education, the losses have been devastating." Low-skilled white males in their twenties had their earnings drop by 14 percent, after adjusting for inflation, between 1973 and 1989. Black males fared worse. Their earnings fell by 24 percent in the same time period.

While millions of urban and rural poor languish in poverty, and an increasing number of suburban middle-income wage earners feel the bite of re-engineering and the impact of technological displacement, a small elite of American knowledge workers, entrepreneurs, and corporate managers reap the benefits of the new high-tech global economy. They enjoy an affluent lifestyle far removed from the social turmoil around them. The frightening new circumstance the United States finds itself in led Secretary of Labor Robert Reich to ask, "What do we owe one another as members of the same society who no longer inhabit the same economy?"

———

From *Economics for a Civilized Society*, by Greg Davidson and Paul Davidson

Pages 115, 116

Keynes's view of entrepreneurial action spurred by "animal spirits" is antithetical to the rational manager envisioned by conservative economics. Accordingly, civilized policy proposals developed on Keynes's analysis are diametrically opposite to the laissez-faire programme advocated by most economists who are fundamentally conservatives.

It is these conflicting views of the entrepreneurial decision-making process which lead to different conclusions regarding the likelihood of free markets to automatically generate job opportunities for all, i.e., for full employment. The conservatives' robot entrepreneurial decision maker is presumed to "know" with actuarial certainty how much output can always fall to the ground under the inevitable natural law of gravity as soon as it releases itself from the branch. Consequently, conservative economists who assume entrepreneurs have rational expectations about future sales conclude that there is no role for government in providing full employment. The authorities can not fool entrepreneurs into hiring more workers than they would already be doing in a laissez-faire environment.

The animal-spirited business manager is the prime mover of any market economic system. In an uncertain world manager decisions regarding productive activities are geared toward a mixture of external incentives (the desire for income) and internal incentives (the desire to accomplish something noteworthy, challenging, and respected by the community). The community, via its cultural and civic values, provides the setting for determining the importance of the various elements in the mix of goals entrepreneurs strive for. In a society where expansive entrepreneurial actions are honoured, the use of expansionary governmental fiscal and monetary policy can create additional profit opportunities that can generate a fully employed citizenry.

The prosperity of any entrepreneurial economic system depends on maintaining an ebullient spirit among managers. Expected increases in demand are necessary to induce managers to hire more workers. On the other hand, pessimistic expectations will cause managers to reduce hiring opportunities. If, at any moment in time, realized sales are just meeting entrepreneurial expectations and if managers project current market conditions into the future, employment will remain unchanged. The economic future is precariously hinged on the psychology of the business decision-maker.

Government therefore can and must take action to influence that psychology. If managers become pessimistic (perhaps because they are disappointed in current market performance), then government has the ability, through its taxation, expenditure, and monetary policies, to stimulate additional demand that will wake entrepreneurs out of their lethargy and encourage economic activity. As long as there are idle workers and unused capacity, the entrepreneurial system is not delivering the goods. It is wasting available resources which could, if employed, improve the well-being of all the citizens of society. It is the responsibility of a central government of a civilized society to create an environment where the system persistently delivers all the goods it is capable of producing.

Published by M.E. Sharpe, Armonk, NY: 1988. Permission Granted, G. Chandoha, Permission Mgr.

———

From *Economics, What Went Wrong, and Why, and Some Things to Do About It*, by George P. Brockway

Pages 2-7

ii

It is a journalistic commonplace that all modern schools of economics, from far left to far right, are in disarray. If this is so, it is because the foundations of the discipline, which were laid in 1776 by Adam Smith, are now crumbling. These foundations were built on by Karl Marx no less than by John Stuart Mill. It has taken two hundred years for cracks in the foundation to become suspect, and it will undoubtedly take a while longer before the suspected cracks are seen, and even longer before it is recognized that they are beyond repair. In the meantime we shall all suffer from recurrent symptoms of unemployment, inflation, and international disorder, while confused teams of economists, businessmen, bankers and statesmen search despairingly for a cure.

Adam Smith was certainly not an isolated figure in the history of thought and we will better understand both his achievement and its limitations if we make at least a provisional attempt to place him in his time. The great movement of which he was a part, and of which we may now be seeing the end, made its first stirring in the natural sciences. Copernicus may conveniently be considered the beginning, though of course many were those who were before him. His dates (1473-1543) roughly coincided with or overlap Piero della Francesca's *Resurrection* and Michelangelo's *Last Judgment*, Columbus' discovery of America, Luther's posting of the ninety-five theses on the door of the Saxon castle church, and the consolidation of nation states in France under Louis XI and Charles VIII and in England under the Tudors. It was a turbulent time, the death of an old world.

Copernicus' contribution was an early glimpse of a rational and impersonal natural world. What he did was only slowly appreciated. It is possible that he himself had an inkling of the dangers inherent in his book on the revolutions of the heavenly bodies, for it was not published until he lay on his deathbed, though he had evidently finished it thirteen years previously. Nevertheless, the book circulated quietly for almost a hundred years before the Church prosecuted Galileo for expounding its ideas. Today, it is often protested that there is no conflict between science and religion, and that the prosecution of Galileo was unnecessary and a strategic mistake. This is an anachronism. The Church was surely prescient in fearing the consequences of a heliocentric universe, and the professors at Padua had good reason to be wary of what they might see if they looked through Galileo's telescope. There was no longer an actual place for Heaven above or for Hell below. In simplifying the harmony of the spheres, Copernicus had put the whole medieval synthesis at risk.

The threat to the Church lay less in the discovery of new facts about the world, startling though they were, than in developing a new way of thinking about the world. Galileo was not the first to demonstrate that Aristotle had been mistaken in teaching that the velocity of falling objects was proportionate to their weight. Simon Stevin, a Dutchman, had done this fifty years before him. But Galileo was the first to derive a mathematical proof of the true velocity of falling objects and then to devise a repeatable experiment that permitted its confirmation. If any single act made modern science possible, it was this. More: it made modern science inevitable.

The three essentials of Galileo's method were abstraction, measurement, and repetition. We are so much his children that we take these for granted and fail to see their wonder. Lacking anything even remotely like a stopwatch, Galileo relied at first on counting his pulse beats in order to measure the time it took for a brass ball to roll down a groove in an inclined plane. Later he devised a sort of water clock that allowed him to measure, "with such exactness," as he said, "that the trials being many and many times repeated, they never differed any considerable matter."

The precision he obtained would have been impossible without abstraction. His "brazen ball, very hard, round, and smooth" was a physical object stripped to its essentials. It did not matter, as he wrote in *Il Saggiatorea*, whether it was "white or red, bitter or sweet, sounding or mute, of a pleasant or unpleasant odor." Thus it was possible to abstract from (disregard) the sense qualities of objects and concentrate on distance and clock time, both of which are measurable, and both of which are factors in the velocity of any moving object whatever.

It also became possible to disregard the occult (that is to say, hidden) qualities of things that medieval philosophers claimed were responsible for physical changes. And Newton wrote, "To tell us that every species of thing is endowed with an occult specific quality, by which it acts and produces manifest effects, is to tell us nothing." The Newtonian laws of motion were neither special nor occult. They applied to everything, from an apple to the moon, even to the Earth itself. They were abstract, concerning distance, which was not a thing but a measure. They were, moreover, timeless. "It seems probable to me," he wrote, "that God in the beginning formed matter in solid, massy, hard, impenetrable, moveable particles. . . as most conduced to the end for which he formed them." Though Newton himself did not take the next step, it was only a short one from his belief to the Deist view of the world as a sort of giant clock that God had invented and built and wound up and left to run of its own accord in obedience to the principles He built into it.

Newton's *Mathematical Principles of Natural Philosophy* was published in 1687, and for the next two hundred-odd years physicists and astronomers were enthusiastically occupied in tracing the works of that giant clock. Copernicus and Galileo had deprived God of an actual place for His Heaven; Galileo and Newton deprived Him of anything to do. At the same time, they deprived priests of much of their revealed authority. If an eclipse of the sun was a natural occurrence it could not be cited as an expression of God's wrath at the sinfulness of mankind. If an eclipse of the sun was not an expression of God's wrath, it became difficult to argue that a plague was, either, and so the way was open to discover the roles of the rat and the flea.

iii

Medieval ethical doctrine, which included medieval economics, concerned a static society in which the proper relations of individual to individual and of individuals to God were immutable. It was a world of six foreordained periods, from Creation to Second Coming, to which St. Augustine had added a seventh, the Eternal Sabbath. Though these periods followed one after the other, they described a sequence, not a history. The various periods had been and would be reached and passed regardless of what anyone did or did not do; and what was virtuous or sinful had no relation to any period but was from everlasting to everlasting.

During the Renaissance, the medieval ban on usury spurred the first tentative steps in the direction of fractional-reserve banking, which, coupled with double-entry bookkeeping, introduced a dynamism into business that was as fateful for the static medieval world view as was the cosmology of Copernicus. After Adam Smith, economic theory, following economic practice, became dynamic. It did so, not by reforming its ethical base, but ultimately by denying it.

In the second chapter of *The Wealth of Nations*, Smith announces that the "division of labor, from which so many advantages are derived, is not originally the effect of any human wisdom. It is the necessary, though very slow and gradual, consequence of a certain propensity in human nature which has in view no such extensive utility as the propensity to truck, barter, and exchange one thing for another." This is clearly the theme of impersonality, but the definitive metaphor does not yet appear.

We hear of the invisible hand in a surprising context. "By preferring the support of domestic products to that of foreign industry, (every individual) intends only his own security; and by directing that industry in such a manner as its produce may be of the greatest value, he intends only his own gain, and he is in this, as in many other cases, led by an invisible hand to promote an end which was no part of his intention. Nor is it always the worse for society that it was no part of it. By pursuing his own interest he frequently promotes that of society more effectually than he really intends to promote it. I have never known much good done by those who affected to trade for the public good. It is affectation indeed, not very common among merchants." Smith adds drily, "and very few words need be employed in dissuading them from it."

There are several aspects of this passage that may be astonishing. First, it comes not at the beginning of the book (where Smith put his famous analysis of the division of labor) but halfway through it, as an incidental point in an argument against import restrictions. Second, it is not stated as an immutable rule (*"Nor is it always the worse,"* *"frequently,"* "I have never known *much* good"). Third, it is based on merchants' preferences (which no longer exist, if they ever did) for domestic over foreign product. Fourth, it is connected with the rest of economics only as an afterthought ("as in many other cases"). Yet the invisible hand shook the world.

Smith's metaphorical, but perhaps as frequently cited, statement of the idea comes even further on, more than two-thirds through the book:

" . . the obvious and simple system of natural liberty establishes itself of its own accord. Every man, as long as he does not violate the laws of justice, is left perfectly free to pursue his own interest in his own way, and to bring both his industry and capital into competition with those of any men or order of men." This comes at the end of an attack on the physiocrats. But now Smith goes on to state explicitly the factor of the idea that gave it its historical power: "The sovereign is completely discarded from a duty . . . for the proper performance of which no human wisdom or knowledge could ever be sufficient: the duty of superintending the industry of private people, and of directing it toward the employments most suitable to the interests of society."

Here Adam Smith had made the wealth of nations seem an impersonal science on the model of Newtonian physics. Thus he changed irrevocably the conditions of our thoughts and lives. His words were so simple, so elegant, so appropriate to the spirit of the times that they carried instant conviction to all who heard them. Where only a few years earlier Rousseau had declared that "Man is born free, and everywhere he is in chains," the striking off of those chains now seemed an imminent possibility. And it would be done automatically, effortlessly, by the invisible hand, now that the heavy hand of sovereign lords was seen to be unnecessary. No one any longer needed to feel guilty in challenging the inherited authority of kings or the revealed morality of priests as obligatory guides. The pursuit of self interest would work, regardless of intention, for the benefit of all; and self-serving labor, freed of its taint of miserliness and greed, could achieve miracles of production, making use of the technical miracles of the natural sciences. The wealth of nations, which had previously been determined by military or dynastic maneuvering, could become the daily concern of commoners.

iv

By Darwin's time the scientific method developed by Galileo was carrying all before it. If every event has a cause, and if the universe is uniform, miracles are no longer sought or feared. Scientific inquiry, once fairly begun, is interminable.

Pages 12, 13

Enlightened self-interest is a dogma no more successful in subduing the riot of human behavior than is self-interest without the enlightenment. Neither can make anything of a man like St. Francis. Was he bartering for his soul when he shed his raiment and renounced his inheritance? What were his worldly contemporaries doing when they bought and sold indulgences? Which of these were enlightened and which misguided cannot be determined by examining their success in reaching their objectives or by assaying the pleasure they enjoyed. It would be preposterous to claim that Gandhi led the Satyagraha in order to enjoy mundane comfort; it would also be preposterous to claim that, had he been enlightened, he would not have led it.

Self-interest as the profit motive is frankly a form of selfishness or greed. Samuel Johnson was willing to say that "There are few ways in which a man can be more innocently employed than in getting money," but sharp practice is not so innocent. While no one praises greed as such, many somehow think that economics can bend it to its purposes.

This is an uncommon state of affairs in the history of civilization and its discontents. In most other cases where a motive is identified, the motive or drive or instinct is judged vicious in its natural state and only becomes beneficent under restraint, if then. Thus unbridled lust would destroy society; so society seeks to control it, not to encourage it. "It is better to marry than to burn," said St. Paul. By its recognition of marriage, society transforms lust into caring and responsibility, if not into love. Even a frequently useful drive, like aggressiveness, is not encouraged to advance to assault, battery, and murder. Many are tempted by the rewards of thievery; some find difficulty in telling the truth, even under oath. These are recognized disorders, and we restrain them with legal sanctions. But the profit motive is assiduously encouraged.

110

The formlessness of the profit motive is underlined by its inability to say what cannot be allowed in its pursuit. The rule of *caveat emptor* is favored because it eases the way of the maker of profits. Some say slavery is inefficient but are still content to recommend the indirect coercion of starvation. Dangerous working conditions that amount to mayhem and manslaughter seem to be not unacceptable if safety measures threaten to interfere with profit making.

Published by Harper and Row, New York, 1985. Permission granted by George P. Brockway.

Chapter 8

POLITICIANS

Government is involved with poverty at every level, city, state, and national. Dealing with poverty engages legislators, administrators, and judges. On each level and branch, government has capacities for making the poverty situation worse or better. We depend on politicians to fulfill the responsibilities of government.

Politicians deal with poverty in numerous ways and each reflects attitudes, concerns, and beliefs held by the public at large. Reviewing how governmental policies are developed, the legislative processes by which programs are designed, and the structures needed to administer and evaluate those programs, can lead us into a whole library of studies, statistics, court cases, historical accounts, and philosophical disputes.

A holistic approach to studying poverty involves exploring why present assumptions, interpretations, policies and programs are so inadequate, and why the vast energies and expense of private and public poverty programs have perpetuated the blight rather than overcoming it. I have contended that the educational establishment of the country has a responsibility to help the public gain a broader understanding of the poverty situation because the public is still largely ignorant of basic causes. I have also examined the role of business and other employers, and the ways they perpetuate rather than overcome poverty.

The poverty-related tasks of government depend upon what educators and employers do or fail to do. It is their failures which now handicap efforts of politicians to both clarify and fulfill their distinctive roles. But like the other power sectors, government, too, attempts to assuage the social damage of poverty while perpetuating it.

Because "government," with its different levels of branches, multiple departments, and endless bureaucracies is so vast, trying to understand its positive or negative functions requires that we first clarify the roles we, the people, have given it. Its role as defender applies to all citizens. Its role of arbiter addresses conflicts among the powerful, both as individuals and as institutions. But government is directly involved with the poor and poverty in its roles of provider and protector.

Government as Provider

Our first impulse when thinking of this role may be to recall what the government had to do in the 1920s and 1930s to overcome the Depression, or what most of us experienced more recently in the midst of the Civil Rights crisis. Before these, in fact from the day Washington was inaugurated, the government has been an employer.

Washington could not have imagined (at least I doubt that he could) that two hundred years later the federal government alone would be employing more than 2.8 million men and women, in addition to 1.4 million employed in the fighting forces. When the employees of states (4.6 million), counties (2.2 million), and cities (2.3 million) are added, the total is more than 13 million. More than ten percent of the total population of the country "lives off the government."

Obviously some of those are the employed poor because there is no secret about the federal pay scale. The bottom grade is G1. According to the U.S. Office of Personnel Management a person with a G1 rating, living in the Washington/Baltimore area, will receive $13,902 in 1998. If a G1 employee is responsible for a family he or she is caught in systemic poverty.

Many federal employees have been successful through their unions in maintaining a decent income, not only for themselves but also for other federal employees. The Congress could be said to have its own union and sees to it that Representatives and Senators do not go hungry.

In some states and cities employees have organized unions that negotiate for decent wages, but in others pay is determined by state legislators, county commissioners, or city council members who do not have to negotiate with workers. Exploring the level of pay in these jurisdictions is one way of finding out how the government closest to us treats those upon whom we depend for common services.

There appears to be little anxiety in the country at this time about levels of government pay (except for those who think Congress receives too much), but the concern is often expressed in comparing the pay of the Secretary of the Treasury with the income of a Wall Street investment CEO, or the salary of a Legal Services lawyer with that of a prominent defense attorney.

The government is most generous to the poor in its role as provider of public education. From the inception of free public education for elementary and high school students, governments on all levels have accepted the responsibility to educate citizens. And they have required that the entire younger population of the country attend school for a prescribed number of days each year. Variations in this major social service have been abundant but the public gives generally favorable support to the principle that children of both the poor and the non-poor have the same claim upon government as their provider of education.

Two additional significant steps have marked the path toward fulfilling that principle. One step is government support of colleges and universities. Adoption of the Morrill Land-Grant College Act of 1862 made it clear that higher education, too, is a government obligation. The other significant step concerned the issue of school segregation by race. It was resolved in principle by the Supreme Court's 1954 decision that separation by race is inherently unequal. Requiring that schools be integrated was a necessary intellectual and social benefit for all children, both poor and non-poor.

In the early 1970s a large group of influential educators and sociologists, supported by the Carnegie and Guggenheim foundations, spent five years in an exhaustive survey, largely statistical, of inequality in schools. As reported in Inequality by Christopher Jencks, the study was an effort to document the effects of schooling on cognitive skills, educational attainment, occupational status, and income. Some general findings are quoted in the For Reflection section of this chapter.

From the time of that study to the present, Jonathan Kozol has been describing, in a series of books, the conditions of schooling in this country, based not on statistics but on his own personal experiences and observations since he started as a teacher in the early 1960s. In his most trenchant account, *Savage Inequality*, published in 1991, Kozol reports in detail on his visits in urban schools across the country where he found that restructuring and reform have made barely a dent in the continuing gap between the schools for the affluent and those for the poor. He found that in city after city teachers and administrators were struggling in crowded classrooms of dilapidated buildings to serve the children of poor neighborhoods, while cheek-by-jowl restructured schools with reformed programs served children of affluent communities. The savagery was the fact that in each instance the two schools were the responsibility of the same board of education.

Government responsibility to provide education for the poor as well as the non-poor has had broad approval. The attitudes and concerns of the public are quite different when considering the government as provider of welfare. The concerns depend upon who receives the "welfare." Usually the term refers to the poor even though with increasing frequency it refers to affluent individuals and corporations.

In the midst of the Depression it was clear, and the public broadly agreed, that the government, and that meant the federal government, should fulfill its role as provider. The public was not quite so clear or supportive of the federal government's later War on Poverty.

Although there is widespread dissatisfaction with the numerous initiatives to deal with specific problems and the number of people administering the programs, welfare for the poor has expanded on both lower and federal levels, because the problems have continued to expand. Present approaches, while keeping many people from starving or living on the street, have not succeeded in addressing the systemic causes of poverty.

As we have noted, all of those initiatives and programs have been grounded on two erroneous assumptions. One is the common view that poverty is caused by the inadequacies and behavior of the poor. The other has been the use of an arbitrary "poverty line" to designate an economic level below which a family is considered to be poor, and above which a family is considered to be out of poverty.

The first of these assumptions has a long history in the West, but as we will find in examining the role of religion, confusion about individual responsibility leads to a very mixed picture. The second error in the use of the poverty line is a recent feature rooted in the need of the government to have a "means test" for determining who should or should not receive assistance the government can provide. It is the government's provider role about which there is the most contention and confusion now. People feel uncertain about what should be provided and who should do the providing.

If and when a living wage policy is adopted it will provide many benefits. There will be a great reduction in the number of poor dependent on governmental and private agencies for help, a serious reduction in the amount of funds now needed to supplement the wages of the employed poor, a sharp decline in the size of the bureaucracies that will be needed to handle the reduced programs, and a major increase in the local economies of cities and counties across the nation.

But most of all a living wage will provide those essential bottom employees with the full benefits of citizenship. It will begin to restore dignity to those who make our lives comfortable, convenient, and profitable. It will make it possible for those employees to choose where they want to live and to eliminate the stigma now visited upon their children when they go to school. And it will open the door for those children and their parents to become more mobile so that they, too, can experience the larger context which the American social and economic landscape provides.

I have no illusions that such a change would take place quickly. Perhaps a decade would be an appropriate time span for the necessary changes to be made. In the process of arriving at real cost accounting for addressing systemic poverty the real cause would then be recognized and acknowledged.

Meanwhile, the government's provider functions must continue to include all of the poor. Children of the employed poor are now consigned to the same world as the children of those who cannot work and those who are not employed outside the home. So far there are significant differences in the results among the states; some accepting the responsibility as an opportunity to do a more effective job of helping the poor, while others use the change to amplify the conviction that people are poor because of their own inadequacies.

There is an interesting parallel between the damaging consequences of large classloads for teachers in poor area public schools and impossibly large client loads for social workers. There are numerous reasons why some poor people cannot work, and different individual needs place a continuing responsibility on public and private agencies to provide a wide range of services. There are also numerous reasons why poor people are not employed, and their individual needs also require specific attention. Smaller caseloads can help agencies provide services more effectively, whether the service is job training, child care, psychological treatment, or other help.

Government is the instrument by which all of us share, through the taxes we pay, in taking care of the needy. This is a crucial task, not only because it serves individuals but also because meeting such needs is essential to a moral civil society. The needy should not be pushed over onto private charity, for then only the benevolent would pay and the rest of us would be "freeloaders."

Government as Protector

The "protector" function of government stems from historical developments, from common beliefs held by members of this society, and from the concept of rights built into our legal structures. Three types of "rights" are involved in current struggles over what the government should protect: property rights, states rights, and human rights.

During the feudal period in Europe, land was "property," and its ownership was often established by royal grants and protected by military action. Vassals were given the use of land in exchange for serving the lord as warriors. As the societies of European nations gradually became industrialized the concept of property expanded to include additional kinds of ownership, such as buildings, machinery, ships, mines, companies, and money.

It is a bit curious that now land property rights are being raised in a new context, and are focused on the "right" of individual landowners against the environmental objectives of governments to protect all citizens. These issues include wetland preservation, air pollution, and zoning regulations. Property rights are an issue also in discussions about contributions to political candidates as some contend that limitations on the use of one's money is a challenge to property rights as well as the right of free speech. The objections made by industry owners to regulations that protect workers (OSHA) and limitations placed on chemical plants that pollute the air and water of nearby poor residential areas are vivid illustrations of property rights impinging on the poor.

On another level there continues to be a deeply held belief that "wealth transfer" from the affluent to the poor violates the rights of the affluent, whatever the mechanism used to carry out that transfer. Similar convictions are held by those who seek to reform the welfare system by cutting funding and programs, but they fail to acknowledge the ways that the government subsidizes business with corporate welfare.

While the idea of property rights was rooted in European developments and predated the founding of this country, our nation's founders saw no reason to respect the property rights of Native Americans. But an early concern about "states rights" has continued and figures strongly in current pressure to leave welfare for the poor to the states.

Philosophers and other scholars have struggled with the issue of "rights" from the time of Locke, Jefferson, Madison, and Hamilton to John Rawls and Charles Murray, and we should be doing the same. Views of rights held by contemporary writers indicate that the struggle goes on.

It was in 1966 that the United Nations adopted the International Bill of Human Rights, but it was 1977 before it was ratified by the United States. One of the earliest acts of the delegates from fifty nations to the UN Charter meeting in San Francisco in 1946 was to set up a Commission on Human Rights. Although the meeting was held in this country and Eleanor Roosevelt was chosen to chair the Commission, no one could have guessed that the Congress would "haggle" (as Peter Meyer described in his history about the Bill) for 41 years before making the commitment to abide by its provisions.[1]

Articles 23-25 of the General Assembly's Universal Declaration of Human Rights provides the setting for this government's protective function:

Article 23

1. Everyone has the right to work, to free choice of employment, to just and favorable conditions of work and to protection against unemployment.

2. Everyone, without any discrimination, has the right to equal pay for equal work.

3. Everyone who works has the right to just and favorable remuneration ensuring for himself and his family an existence worthy of human dignity, and supplemented, if necessary, by other means of social protection.

4. Everyone has the right to form and to join trade unions for the protection of his interests.

Article 24

Everyone has the right to rest and leisure, including reasonable limitations of working hours and periodic holidays with pay.

Article 25

1. Everyone has the right to a standard of living adequate for the health and well-being of himself and of his family, including food, clothing, housing and medical care, necessary social services, and the right to security in the event of unemployment, sickness, disability, widowhood, old age, or other lack of livelihood in circumstances beyond his control.

2. Motherhood and childhood are entitled to special care and assistance. All children, whether born in or out of wedlock, shall enjoy the same social protection.

It is interesting that while the United Nations General Assembly framed these objectives as "protection," and America now emphasizes human rights in foreign policy, within the country we still tolerate a wide gap between declaration and protection of our own citizens.

It should be obvious that the employed poor have no other recourse than the power of government to protect the rights to which this country subscribes. The UN General Assembly declaration on Human Rights began with a statement that, "all nations . . . every individual and every organ of society . . . shall strive . . to secure their universal and effective recognition and observance."

The extent to which such rights are "secured" varies among the states, but neither we nor the poor are "citizens" of states; we are all citizens of the nation. The national government has both the power and the means for the protection it should be enforcing nationwide. At least three "means" are available and have often been employed in other contexts: regulation, arbitration, and condemnation, and all of these can have direct impact in protecting the poor.

As a vehicle for implementing the will of the people, government is an arena in which ideological, political, religious, and cultural commitments are in continuous contention. In considering what we should do about systemic poverty we need to remember how governmental processes reflect our social concerns. We need to remind ourselves of what we already know. We know that implementation of any one of the "human rights" spelled out by the Universal Declaration of Human Rights depends on some Senator or Representative introducing a bill that is adopted by the Congress and signed by the President. Objections to implementation of that bill may eventually require action by the Supreme Court, or may be revised by further congressional action, or may become part of the platform of a candidate for office.

We also know that actions taken by the legislative, administrative, or judicial arms of the federal, state or local governments, are not permanent devices. Political solutions to problems of poverty, as to problems in other domains, depend on the continuing exercise of power and influence. Actions that have popular support can be reversed when the public mood changes, as has been illustrated with affirmative action.

Obviously this country has already gone beyond formal approval and put into practice many of the guidelines proposed by the Universal Declaration, but the question remains: what could generate sufficient pressure to implement all of the human rights to which formal approval has been given by this country? Our assumption is that the power centers of this society are so interrelated that realism requires simultaneous solutions.

If changes are to be made we, the nonpoor, have to change the system. Leading the change will be those of us who have the decency to admit that we should no longer claim "affirmativae actiosn" for ourselves at the expense of the poor. It will be those who are willing to recognize that we have received more than we deserve. This will be done when both individuals and corporations recognize upon whom they depend.

* * * * *

FOR REFLECTION

From *Inequality, A Reassessment of the Effect of Family and Schooling in America*, by Christopher Jencks

Page 3

During the 1960s, many reformers devoted enormous effort to equalizing opportunity. More specifically, they tried to eliminate inequalities based on skin color, and to a lesser extent on economic background. They also wanted to eliminate absolute deprivation: "poverty," "ignorance," "powerlessness," and so forth. But only a handful of radicals talked about eliminating inequality per se. Almost none of the national legislation passed during the 1960s tried to reduce disparities in adult status, power, or income in any direct way. There was no significant effort, for example, to make taxation more progressive, and very little effort to reduce wage disparities between the highly paid and poorly paid workers. Instead, attention focused on helping 0workers in poorly paid jobs to move into better paid jobs.

Page 11

Our commitment to equality is, then, neither all-embracing nor absolute. We do not believe that everyone can or should be made equal to everyone else in every respect. We assume that some differences in cognitive skill and vocational competence are inevitable, and that efforts to eliminate such differences can never be 100 percent successful. But we also believe that the distribution of income can be made far more equal than it is, even if the distribution of cognitive skill and vocational competence remains as unequal as it is now. We also think society should get on with the task of equalizing income rather than waiting for the day when everyone's earning power is equal.

Page 253

We found that both genetic and environmental inequality played a major role in producing cognitive inequality. We also found that those who started life with genetic advantages tended to get environmental advantages as well, and that this exacerbated inequality.

We began by looking at the distribution of educational opportunity. We found that access to school resources was quite unequal. Schools in some districts and neighborhoods spend far more than schools in other neighborhoods. We also found that utilization of school resources was even more unequal than access to them at least after the age of 16.

Page 254

We found that family background had much more influence than IQ genotype on an individual's educational attainment. The family's influence depended partly on its socio-economic status and partly on cultural and psychological characteristics that were independent of socio-economic level.

Pages 255, 256

None of the evidence we have reviewed suggests that school reform can be expected to bring about significant social changes outside the schools. More specifically, the evidence suggests that equalizing educational opportunity would do very little to make adults more equal.

There seem to be three reasons why school reform cannot make adults more equal. First, children seem to be far more influenced by what happens at home than by what happens in school. They may also be more influenced by what happens on the streets and by what they see on television. Second, reformers have very little control over those aspects of school life that affect children. Reallocating resources, reassigning pupils, and rewriting the curriculum seldom change the way teachers and students actually treat each other minute by minute. Third, even when a school exerts an unusual influence on children, the resulting changes are not likely to persist into adulthood. It takes a huge change in elementary school test scores, for example, to alter adult income by a significant amount.

Looking at schooling as an end in itself rather than a means to some other end suggests that we ought to describe schools in a language appropriate to a family rather than to a factory. This implies that we will have to accept diverse standards for judging schools, just as we do for judging families. Indeed, we can even say that diversity should be an explicit objective of schools and school systems.

Published by Basic Books, New York, 1972. Passages used by permission.

From *Persons, Rights, and the Moral Community,* by Loren E.
   Lomasky

Page 131

The theory of basic rights cannot view communities as vast
agglomerations of *tabulae rasae* waiting to be written on by an
authorized seer or social unit. Persons come to civil society with ends
that are theirs, however those ends were generated and shaped. The
system of moral and legal rights that are socially determined in society
must respect the ends that persons have rather than assert a baseless
authority collectively to determine what ends persons have reason to
pursue. Similarly, persons come to civil society with things that are
theirs. A socially defined system of property rights must be responsive
to what persons have. In no respect does a civil order entail the
collectivization of property which is then available to be doled out to
persons according to social plan.

Page 141

Although rights must not be violated, they will be. That is the
unavoidable accompaniment of social life in an imperfect world,
imperfect with regard to the moral character of individuals and with
respect to the information that persons have. Even if all persons be
maximally conscientious, infringements of rights would still occur as the
result of inadvertence. The theory of basic rights must, then, include
provisions for response to acts that intrude on moral space.

From *Moral Imagination and Public Life,* by Thomas E.
   McCollough.

Pages 26, 27

124

With the dissolution of traditional ties of medieval community, the individual was liberated to stand alone, with a sense both of new powers and of greater vulnerability to forces of the marketplace. The common social world was divided into autonomous realms of science, religion, economics, and politics, each seen as self-regulating. The rise of the scientific outlook brought a new way of looking at the world, as an alien reality bereft of human meaning but subject to human control. Human reason was conceived more and more as technical rationality, limited to calculations of the most efficient means, leaving ends or purposes to individual preferencee. The common standard of value became utility, seen succesively as happiness, pleasure, individual interest, and money. Value was sundered from fact, eliminated from the realms of science and economics and, in the political realm, equated with individual interest. It is against the background of these developments that modern social theory is to be understood. We may then see why it is difficult to raise the ethical question in the public realm.

The pathfinding thinkers of the Enlightement could take for gratned the moral-communal background of social life, no matter how critical their theories might be of the social bonds of community, authority, and religion. . .

Pages 88, 89

In contrast with policy making based on interest-group inter-mediation and net benefit maximization, public deliberation allows people to discuss ideas, discover shared values, and recognize deeper conflicets that need to be confronted and resolved. The public interest is then more than neutral, procedural policy making. It is deliberation by citizens about public values.

If citizens are not able or willing to think about these matters and to hold their political represeentatives responsible for informed moral judgments about them, decision making will be left to a few people in strategic positions. Their power will grow in direct proportion to the degree of secrecy cloaking their decisions. It will not be the power to act for the good of all, however, but for their own benefit. Unchecked by reference to moral norms or popular will, power will tend to be exploited for private purposes. Public issue call for communal lifeworld perspective, both to understand the issues in their proper context and to respond to them as matters affecting the well-being of the whole community. To leave our corporate fate to a self-interested elite of specialists and politicians is to forfeit our responsibilities of citizenship and make way for an authoritative government. Liberalism's equation of values with interests and its identification of interest-group pluralism with democratic policy making leaves no basis for raising the ethical question. But the issues facing us require ethical judgment, that in turn depends on public morality, a commitment to public values transcending narrow self-interest. To hold ourselves accountable to others for what we know and say and do is to create the public.

Chapter 9

CLERGY

Religion and poverty have kept company for many centuries, through many different kinds of relationship.

In the modern era, when concerned and benevolent people of religious persuasion have encountered poverty their religious impulses have prompted numerous efforts to help the poor. But two interesting characteristics puzzle those who attempt to examine the relationship of religion to poverty. One puzzle is how to make sense of the long religious tradition in which poverty has often been held as a virtue. The other is trying to explain how the different social roles of poverty relate to the social roles of religion.

Most societies accommodate a religious sector that incorporates two quite different views of religion, the historic and the civic. In some societies the historic religious communities share characteristics with the larger cultural context, in others the religious traditions dominate and shape all aspects of culture, and in still others some or all formal religions are considered to be subversive to the surrounding society.

In most societies there are also "civic religions" which express human commitments to many other values than those which characterize the major historic religious traditions. To fully understand the relation of religion and poverty it is important to examine both types of religion.

So far in the United States the dominant formal historic religious traditions have been Judaism and two branches of Christianity, Catholic and Protestant. As the number of followers of Islam, Buddhism, Shinto, and Hinduism increase the religious pluralism of this society, their impact may grow as well.

Of the three dominant traditions, certain portions of Protestantism have exerted the most direct influence on the cultural development of this society, but all three share roots that reach back many centuries. Each tradition is a rhetorical universe, with its own sanctified literary and verbal formulations which bind its adherents together. Each tradition is built around institutional structures to which its adherents belong and which they support. Each tradition has developed a set of behaviors and actions that are expected or required of all adherents.

Rhetoric

"In the beginning was the Word, and the Word was with God, and the Word was God." So wrote the author of the Gospel of John in the New Testament. Words have special significance for a religion of The Book. Rhetoric expresses sets of beliefs, provides comfort, directs worship, gives form to prayers. In fact special words facilitate every phase of religious activity.

Our concern is with the religious meaning given to the words "poor" and "poverty," and how they become sets of beliefs promoted in books, periodicals, and official pronouncements about the theological and ethical positions of religious bodies, and which become a major content in their religious education programs.

A major illustration of dealing with the issues of poverty is *Economic Justice for All*, a Pastoral Letter issued in 1986 by the U.S. Bishops of the Roman Catholic Church, a document on which they had been working for many years. One feature of the Letter is its review of numerous passages in the Bible which describe the conditions of the poor and what should be done to help them. These passages lay the groundwork for principles and policy recommendations. See the For Reflection of this chapter for excerpts.

In both the Old and New Testaments the term "poor" may connote the poor in spirit, people with whom others need to identify, those without material things, or those who are blessed because they have not been corrupted by wealth. Biblical scholars and exegetes have examined, debated, argued, even voted about seemingly every possible interpretation of biblical passages, including those that refer to poverty and the poor. This extended consideration has been necessary because different religious traditions emphasize different passages of scripture, and also because these are ancient texts employed long before the industrial age gave very different meanings to the language we use to talk about the poor and poverty.

Another illustration of attempts in the 1980s to formulate a religious approach to understanding and dealing with poverty is the two-year effort of an interdenominational organization, Church Women United. Their publication *Perfect Charity Brings Forth Justice* has this introduction:

> This is a resource for all those committed to eliminating the root causes of poverty of women and children. For years we have been involved in helping those who are poor. Now the situation is so precarious that we must go beyond helping the victims: we must do away with whatever causes poverty. But the poor need us to continue helping them in order to survive. What we need to do, then, is to continue to feed the hungry, comfort the afflicted, clothe the naked, shelter the homeless, defend the abused, while at the same time challenging the oppressive structures which cause poverty and injustice. Only then will justice, charity made perfect, flourish.

The publication's contents are listed in the For Reflection section.

The word "poverty" appears just 15 times in the King James translation of the Bible and its reference is to conditions of individuals in a context vastly different from today. Translating the meaning of the term into the experiences of men, women, and children in industrial societies can be confusing. Nevertheless, the present meaning is assumed in the pronouncements, social action documents, and organized discussions of such matters.

Most mainline churches and synagogues employ such documents to assist leaders and adherents in thinking about the ethical implications in the modern setting of common biblical demands for justice. Making clear the "causes of poverty" called for by Church Women United is not easy.

A Cry for Justice, The Churches and Synagogues Speak, edited by Robert McAfee Brown and Sydney Thomson Brown, is a review by

Jewish and Christian scholars of numerous "pronouncements" on social issues by 19 Catholic, Protestant, and Jewish organizations, 12 of them having issued statements specifically on poverty.

One of the contributors to the book, John Oliver Wilson, focuses on "Justice and Corporate America," comparing Catholic and Protestant approaches. "The basic difference between the achievement of economic justice in the Protestant model and the Catholic model is that the former attempts to achieve justice through a redistribution of economic output after the fact of production of that output (the major reason corporations are excluded from the analysis) while the latter views the achievement of justice as an integral part of the process of participation in the economic system itself (the reason for the overall inclusiveness of the Catholic model)."[22]

Probably the most frequently quoted biblical reference to the poor is Jesus saying (usually employing the King James translation!), "The poor ye shall have with you always," which can often be used as an escape from both study and action.

Poor is always a relative concept, whether used in the first or twentieth century. Poor can mean quite different things depending on the economic status of individuals sitting together in the same church or synagogue. The terms find their way repeatedly into the liturgy of the mass and other church forms of worship. And those weekly gatherings offer the clergy, in their sermons, the greatest opportunity for considering the religious meaning of poor and poverty, and their implications for adherents.

There are no data on how often the clergy include consideration of poverty or justice in their sermons, or what they say about them, nor what effects those sermons have on the awareness or conscience of worshippers. What does seem clear is that references to poverty in Bible study, official statements, liturgical practices, and clergy sermons is that charity is the common expression of religious concern for the poor.

Institutions

What is often absent from the official rhetoric, whether statements adopted by official bodies or by organizations set up specifically to deal with poverty is, as Wilson pointed out, an analysis of institutional arrangements which perpetuate the conditions being criticized. The 1986 Pastoral Letter is an exception, for it devoted a major section to "challenges to the Church" with a blunt statement: "All the moral principles that govern the just operation of any economic endeavor apply to the church and its agencies and institutions; indeed the church should be exemplary."

Seldom do most pronouncements examine the salary policies of churches or synagogues to see if their employees are receiving a living wage. What do they pay "the help" that prepares meals, cleans buildings, maintains the office, etc.? It is curious, however, that the Pastoral Letter does not deal with the historic requirement that "the religious" take a vow of poverty. It is also interesting that the monumental document with its extensive descriptions of conditions that should be met, gives very little attention to examining the basic causes of those conditions.

For centuries religious organizations have addressed the poor with services of many kinds. Even during the feudal period in Europe there were people not tied to the land and the manor system who were homeless and jobless, who wandered from country to country, whom we might call vagabonds, for whom church related organizations were the only source of help. St. Francis of Assisi and Sisters of Charity cared for the sick, for foundlings, for the dispossessed. As the feudal arrangements were being replaced in England the government turned to churches to take care of paupers and itinerants.

According to Michael Rose in his *The English Poor Law 1780-1930*,

> The act of 1601 made it compulsory for each parish to provide for the poor by levying a rate on all occupiers of property within its bounds. An unpaid parish officer, the overseer of the poor, was to be appointed. His duties were to levy and collect the rate and to see that it was expended in the relief of the aged and infirm poor, the apprenticing to a trade of the children of paupers, and the "settling on work" of the able-bodied poor.

This principle of compulsory provision made the English poor law system unique, marking it off even from Scotland and Ireland where no such provision existed until the nineteenth century.[23]

It did not take long for them to discover that the resources of churches were not up to the job. However, Rose reports that Lyons, in France, was the first government entity to reverse course and place the responsibility for assistance to the poor on the city government.

Although the American scene is very different, since there is no state church as in European countries, the proliferation of religion-grounded social services, though vast, now forces recognition that here, too, the resources of churches are not up to the job. There is no possibility of religious charities taking the place of government-supported welfare.

But the limited capacity of churches in dealing with poverty has deeper causes than their resources for social services. In this country most religious bodies are "class identified." Some serve a particular ethnic membership, but even among these the geographical location of churches and synagogues has meant that if they are in suburbia they are identified with the upper classes while those in central city are more likely to be located among, and serve, the poor.

Similarly, the "class" of their members is also reflected in the polity and organizational structures of religious bodies. Except in Catholic, Episcopal, and Methodist churches, local congregations control the selection of pastors and determine their responsibilities. The more democratic the polity the more likely it is that the orientation and social views of religious leaders is shared with (controlled by in some instances) the socio-economic class to which the membership belongs.

Churches proclaim their identity, often unintentionally, by their architecture as well as by their organization and pronouncements. The location, materials, style, and size of buildings used by religious institutions usually express a particular socio-economic relationship. True, a wealthy donor may have endowed a magnificent edifice in what has since become a slum area so that the old building now provides shelter for a welter of community groups and activities. In that case, the building may say more about its past than about the present, still identifying its class origins.

What churches teach unintentionally can contribute to ambiguity. As religious institutions, they claim a special concern for the sacred and at the same time claim a special status in society, such as in taxes. The public, remembering the moving rhetoric that was used when each church or agency was established, later witnesses the inevitable shift of emphasis from service to survival, keeping the institution going. Every church body is constantly preoccupied with gaining members, and most churches are also pragmatic in measuring success by the number of adherents and attendance. Because of the constant pressure on institutionalized religion by the general culture, there is little likelihood that the traditional churches in the United States will lead any reconstruction of the society and its culture. The ambivalence of their teaching, not realizing how unrelated what they advocate with their right hand is to what they do with their left, gives scant hope to those who would like to see churches and synagogues as vigorous agents for change, as bellwethers for a more just and responsible society.

Action

Church Women United indicated a hope that charity would lead to justice, that the right hand would work in harmony with the left, but in addressing poverty the actions of both hands need reexamination, for charity is often the major barrier to justice.

Catholic, Jewish, and Protestant religious institutions have been creative in developing programs to help the poor, and for years have maintained those programs in every part of the country. As the Church Women contended, while working for justice the poor still need food and housing. But at the same time they fail to recognize how charity stands in the way of justice.

Taking the Good Samaritan parable as a guide to religious duty misses the point. The Samaritan helped the robbed traveler but that did not lead to organizing a system for effective policing of the highway so that travelers would be protected from robbers. Aiding the victim does not change the victimizing system.

We have all heard the simple observation that instead of being given fish the poor should be taught to fish for themselves. The idea is simplistic, because it is additional evidence that charitable people still believe the cause of poverty is individual inadequacy.

Charity is an omnibus word, referring to all sorts of activities. There are charity balls raising funds for museums, and contributions to a club's Christmas collection of toys to be given away, not knowing who needs what. Christmas is the one time of the year that offers so many opportunities by all kinds of organizations to dramatize their virtue, as if the needy could get along without until next December.

Charity gets confused with benevolence: is it charity that we put in a collection plate, a benevolence, or a payment on a pledge? What about the quarter we drop in a beggar's hat? And every April 15th our honesty is challenged as we list our deductions, and some feel that most of their tax payments are used as charity for the undeserving. Or what of our response to the urgent plea of our alma mater, is that a charity or repayment of a debt? Do any of these contribute toward a just society?

Charles A. Summers, writing in the *Presbyterian Outlook*, in 1981, contended that charity is a far more comfortable concept than justice.

> It has many fine selling points. Charity is voluntary. . . A man wrote to the editor of the *Presbyterian Survey* concerning food stamps: "The system is a disgrace to our heritage and an insult to the people who pay for it. The good Lord provides food for the birds but he doesn't toss it into their nests. All charity should be voluntary, not forced upon the taxpayers."
>
> Second, charity makes us feel good about ourselves. It draws a picture of us as generous. . .It assuages our guilt over how much we do have. For we can always point to the things we have given away.
>
> Third, charity asks no embarrassing questions. If the madam at the brothel wants to make a donation to the Boy Scouts, that is fine. . . If a realtor in the congregation suddenly triples his income and his pledge, no one asks about condo conversions or block-busting practices.
>
> Charity is to American religion what ritual sacrifice was to

Israel. In the days of Isaiah, Micah, and Amos there was a great gap between the rich and the poor; and the rich folk were very religious. . . They were a pious people, but not a just people.[24]

Charity is an exercise of power. We decide what the needy will receive, how much, and when. We also determine the conditions to be met before they can receive. All of this is demeaning for the needy, whether applying for food stamps, accessing the church's clothes closet, or asking for a meal at the soup kitchen. That sad relationship: on one side of the counter is the needy one feeling miserable because he or she is hungry and has to ask, and on the other side we hand out the food or clothes feeling good about what we are doing, sure that we are meeting an obvious need. . . But even if we do not feel especially virtuous, are genuinely concerned, are committed to setting aside the time and energy to help, that does not change the demeaning experience for those on the other side of the counter, including those who in need demand rather than ask. They are kept dependent.

The other sad relationship is when charity is lifted from the individual and personal level to public policy, causing us to resent the demand that we pay for it in taxes, so we blame the victims for depending on us. Forgetting how much we depend on the poor, we look only at their dependence. Ivan Illich has lifted this to an even larger scope and calls it "the seamy side of charity" when generosity gratuitously offered imposes a burden on the recipient. Seeing this happen "is to taste the bitterness of the damage done by our sacrifice."[25]

A policy which makes charity central to meeting the needs of the poor is unjust because it expects the benevolent to do what all of us should be doing together. This is unfair; it only perpetuates the patterns of injustice which we have inherited. To attain justice is to overcome injustice. We do not begin with a blank slate but belong to a country that is explicitly committed to liberty and justice for all.

In this commitment our Judeo-Christian inheritance is exposed. The Hebrew prophets and Jesus made it clear that justice was a human requirement central to their religion. Amos said "let justice roll down like waters, and righteousness like an everflowing stream" (5:24), and

Matthew reported that Jesus made it very personal, "So whatever you wish that men would do to you, do so to them, for this is the law and the prophets" (7:12).

The Judeo-Christian tradition has had a profound impact in shaping our past, and justice is a keystone of that tradition. The prophets were shrewd observers of their times and recognized how difficult it would be to attain a just society. We, often glibly, repeat the pledge but there is a serious tension between the claim of liberty and the claim of justice. Part of our liberty, we feel, should be freedom to be charitable, to decide what we want to give and to whom, and to hold certain expectations of recipients, these as evidences of our liberty. How then can we meet the two basic moral demands, and be both charitable and just, at the same time?

These are both valid but are not equal claims; the need for charity is the more obvious of the two. The need for justice does not seem to be so insistent as we share with other non-poor people advantages and opportunities not available to the poor. We seldom stand aside to look at our privileges to see that we benefit greatly from a system that keeps those who do essential bottom jobs from enjoying the fruits of their labor; we are the ones who enjoy those fruits. By paying them less than it costs them to live they are forced to survive by seeking our charity.

When government welfare programs are seen as charity, deserved or undeserved, it cements the barrier to justice. Our energy and concern are engaged with only part of the problem. Justice thus becomes very difficult to grasp, is far easier to say than to do. Of course we want it for ourselves but are lax in making certain it is assured for others. Justice takes away from us the power to determine who will receive our charity. Justice is a problem in many spheres but here we are considering economic justice and we know one evidence of injustice in this society is the tremendous gap between the haves and the have-nots. Justice has to be a collective attainment, for unless it is for all it is not justice.

Although unclear what it may be in every individual and social relationship, it is clear that struggling for justice is a central requirement of our religious tradition.

Other Religions

Churches and synagogues are "religious" institutions, but church and religion can connote quite different domains. In *Theology and Culture*, published in 1959, Paul Tillich pointed out that "religion is being ultimately concerned about that which is and should be our ultimate concern. This means that faith is the state of being grasped by an ultimate concern."[26]

We may repeat the formulas of our religious tradition and feel that they express our genuine beliefs, not realizing that what actually comes first in our lives are other things: our business, our party, our ethnic group, our violin, our job. Any one of these can become our ultimate concern.

The prophet Isaiah charged that putting faith in such things is a form of idolatry, and pointed to those who were regular temple worshippers but for whom their ultimate concerns were more mundane and practical things, "they bow down to the work of their hands, to what their own fingers have made" (2:8). Jeremiah provides a more dramatic analogy, "A tree from the forest is cut down, and worked with an axe by the hands of a craftsman. Men deck it with silver and gold; they fasten it with hammer and nails so it cannot move. Their idols are like scarecrows in a cucumber field" (10:4,5).

When the Conseco Corporation advertises its advice, REFORM AN INDUSTRY, MAKE PERFORMANCE A RELIGION, AND ACHIEVE UNPRECEDENTED SUCCESS THROUGH NONTRADITIONAL MEANS, what is their god? When football players kneel in midfield for prayer (to whom, for what?) before beginning their less than gentle game, what kind of religion is that? And what about the popular college president who, when challenged about his desire to have a Protestant team that could beat Notre Dame, responded, "but Jesus was a winner," what bible was he quoting?

Human beings have elevated many different aspects of their life experience to the sacred. Probably no culture can be adequately understood without taking into account the character of its multiple religiously held values, myths, symbols, buildings, objects, places, and

138

rituals. In a sense all of us are syncretists, that is, we have several concerns to which we are committed: family, party, church, company, art, money, success. All are worthy, but if we had to choose, which would be our ultimate concern? Do any of these call for justice?

The poverty system is one result of the worship of "the market" in the economic sphere and of identification by class in the religious. In other words, whether put in terms of traditional institutions or of contemporary concerns, being comfortable with the poverty system is basically religious. Overcoming the poverty system challenges our basic beliefs.

* * * * *
FOR REFLECTION

A brief summary of the document
Economic Justice for All
Catholic Social Teaching
and the U.S. Economy
(paragraphs are numbered)

The Pastoral Message

Brothers and sisters in Christ: 1. We are believers called to follow our Lord Jesus Christ and proclaim his Gospel in the midst of a complex and powerful economy. This reality poses both opportunities and responsibilities for Catholics in the United States. Our faith calls us to measure this economy not only by what it produces, but also by how it touches human life and whether it protects or undermines the dignity of the human person. . .

2. . . This letter is a personal invitation to Catholics in the United States to use the resources of our faith, the strength of our economy, and the opportunities of our democracy to shape a society that better protects the dignity and basic rights of our sisters and brothers, both in this land and around the world.

Principal Themes of the Pastoral Letter

12. The pastoral letter . . . turns to Scripture and to the social teachings of the Church . . . Let us examine some of these basic moral principles.

13. *Every economic decision and institution must be judged in light of whether it protects or undermines the dignity of the human person.*

14. *Human dignity can be realized and protected only in community.*

15. *All people have a right to participate in the economic life of society.*

16. *All members of society have a special obligation to the poor and vulnerable.*

17. *Human rights are the minimum conditions for life in community.*

18. Society as a whole, acting through public and private institutions, has the moral responsibility to enhance human dignity and protect human rights.

CHAPTER 1. The Church and the Future of the U.S. Economy
   A. The U.S. Economy Today: Memory and Hope
   B. Urgent Problems of Today
   C. The Need for Moral Vision

CHAPTER 2. The Christian Vision of Economic Life
   A. Biblical Perspectives
   B. Ethical Norms for Economic Life
      67b. . . These norms state the minimum levels of mutual care and respect that all persons owe to each other in an imperfect world. Catholic social teaching, like much philosophical reflection, distinguishes three dimensions of basic justice: commutative justice, distributive justice, and social justice.

(Footnote 14. J. Dupont and A. George, eds., La pauvrete evangelique (Paris: Cerf, 1971); M. Hengel, Property and Riches in the Early Church (Philadelphia: Fortress Press, 1974); L. Johnson, Sharing Possessions: Mandate and Symbol of Faith (Philadelphia: Fortress Press, 1981); D.L. Mealand, Poverty and Expectation in the

Gospels (London: SPCK, 1980); W. Pilgrim, *Good News to the Poor: Wealth and Poverty in Luke-Acts* (Minneapolis:Augsburg, 1981); and W. Stegemann, *The Gospel and the Poor* (Philadelphia: Fortress Press, 1984)

70. . . *Distributive justice requires that the allocation of income, wealth, and power in society be evaluated in the light of its effects on persons whose basic material needs are unmet.*

C. Working for Greater Justice: Persons and Institutions

D. Christian Hope and the Courage to Act

CHAPTER 3. Selected Economic Policy Issues

A. Employment

136. Full employment is the foundation of a just economy. . . Our emphasis on this goal is based on the conviction that human work has a special dignity and is a key to achieving justice in society.

B. Poverty

173. By poverty, we are referring here to the lack of sufficient material resources required for a decent life.

196. *The first line of attack against poverty must be to build and sustain a healthy economy that provides employment opportunities at just wages for all adults who are able to work.*

199. *Vigorous action should be undertaken to remove barriers to full and equal employment for women and minorities.*

202. *The tax system should be continually evaluated in terms of its impact on the poor.*

203. *All of society should make a much stronger commitment to education for the poor.*

206. *Policies and programs at all levels should support the strength and stability of families, especially those adversely affected by the economy.*

210. *A thorough reform of the nation's welfare and income-support programs should be undertaken.*

C. Food and Agriculture

D. The U.S. Economy and the Developing Nations: Complexity, Challenge and Choices

CHAPTER 4. A New American Experience: Partnership for the Public
Good
  A. Cooperation Within Firms and Industries
  B. Local and Regional Cooperation
  C. Partnership in the Development of National Policies
  D. Cooperation at the International Level

CHAPTER 5. A Commitment to the Future
  A. The Christian Vocation in the World Today
  B. Challenges to the Church
    347. *All the moral principles that govern the just operation of any
economic endeavor apply to the church and its agencies and institutions;
indeed the Church should be exemplary.*
    350. We select here five areas for special reflection: (1) wages and
salaries, (2) rights of employees, (3) investments and property, (4) works
of charity, and (5) working for economic justice.
  C. The Road Ahead
    360. In this respect we mentioned the twofold aim of this pastoral
letter: to help Catholics form their consciences on the moral dimensions
of economic decision making and to articulate a moral perspective in the
general societal and political debate that surrounds these questions.
  D. Commitment to a Kingdom of Love and Justice

———

From *Perfect Charity Brings Forth Justice, A Church Women United
  Resource Booklet*
  The issues addressed by Church Women United, with both description
and recommended actions included in each section, were:

Hunger	Criminal Justice
Refugees/Immigrants	Environment/Pollution
Advocacy for the Poor	Clothing for the Naked
Childcare	Jobs
Education	Racism

142

Women's Health Care   Elderly Women
Women and Child Abuse   Homelessness

The introduction described the document's function adding, "some of the questions and strategies in this booklet apply to men as well."

One of the more trenchant statements in the document was included in the section on homelessness.

"A thorough-going explanation of homelessness, finding its roots in the housing system, changes in employment patterns, and the spatial restructuring of cities, all abetted by governmental policies, has clear policy implications. First and foremost, homelessness must be seen as component, an extreme reflection, of general social, economic, and political patterns, not as an isolated problem, separate and apart.

"The homeless deserve priority, particularly in access to housing programs. But limiting housing provision just to meeting their immediate needs is self-defeating. The characteristics of the housing system that produces homelessness will continue producing it. . . Other services may be needed, and they may be needed in unusual concentration because of the devastating conditions to which the homeless have had to adapt in the past. Decent housing for the homeless within a decent housing system must meet these needs, just as the special housing needs of women, the elderly, single-parent households, children, and other groups within the population must be met. If housing means homes for all, not just shelter, then the homeless need homes, just like the rest of us.

"Government actions aggravating homelessness must be turned around. . . The system must provide enough decent housing for low-income people, or the problems of homelessness will simply reproduce itself endlessly. To ask the private housing industry to provide such housing where it is not profitable to do so is going against the nature of the beast."

Peter Marcuse, in *Christianity & Crisis*, April 18, 1988. This document was neither dated nor copyrighted.

Chapter 10

ADDRESSING THE POVERTY SYSTEM

There is no simple panacea for America's poverty system. It is intertwined with the total cultural and industrial development of the country. Making necessary changes will take time, but change can and must come. And the changes will be led by those educators, employers, politicians, and clergy who understand both its causes and its damaging social costs. The system is maintained by us, the non-poor, whom it benefits. We need to admit that there is a troubling tension within us between our desire for privileges and our desire for justice.

We can choose one or the other, or we can try to balance them as we carry on our professional, social, and family responsibilities. Neither we nor the institutions of this society are fated to perpetuate a social arrangement that blights the lives of those upon whom it depends. There are things every one of us, every organization in which we work, every association with which we are identified, every religious body in which we participate, and every government unit for which we vote, that we can and should do to fulfill the pledge we keep making to the flag, "with liberty and justice for all."

In what follows we will be looking back and repeating or expanding on ideas already explored to see their implications for action, but we will also consider other suggestions for action and the kinds of barriers that make such action difficult.

Where Are We Now?

It might be interesting to review our own reactions to thinking about the poverty system. This is a personal matter and it may help to ask ourselves such questions as: Has attempting to make a study of poverty provided a new perspective on the problem? How do I now judge the value and importance of the jobs the employed poor do? Do I still accept the argument that pay is low because the jobs require low skill? Am I justified in contending that such jobs have low status because most of them have been seen as "women's work"? Do I agree that having to depend on charity is demeaning?

If we believe we have responsibility to do something about poverty from a different perspective than we held before, and if we are wondering what specific things we can do, how about examining such aspects of our local situation as pay scales for those who do bottom jobs in the businesses we patronize, the views of poverty presented in the newspaper we read, and the attitudes about the poor we hear expressed by friends and acquaintances.

This kind of exploration can be extended, but as we discover the practices of our own surroundings we can, almost automatically, see things to do. Some may be actions we can handle alone, but it is usually more interesting, more carefully considered, and easier to keep at it if we have one or two like-minded friends with whom we share the tasks.

Institutions

Every responsible organization, whether academic, industrial, governmental, or religious, is caught also in the tension between privilege and justice. They all perpetuate poverty but also are primary instruments for movements toward a more just society. All of us are involved with institutions, either as employees, members, supporters, or officers. Every institution has boards and committees, and we may be on several at the same time. Nearly every institution employs the poor for bottom jobs and someone decides how those workers will be treated and paid.

As members of those boards and committees we have a voice in the discussions that lead to decisions. We can make a difference. If a committee we are on recommends or determines pay scales we can suggest consideration of a long-range approach similar to a college which raised salaries of those at the top 5 percent and of those at the bottom

18 percent. If such an approach is continued for several years those bottom level workers will eventually be receiving a living wage.

The board or committee on which we serve may have responsibilities for education, but has never dealt with the problem of poverty and economic justice. Everyone is familiar with the traditional ways of helping the poor, but few have been helped to focus on the other track, dealing with social causes. For many this may be their first opportunity to gain a broader view of our crucial national blight.

Educators

All of us are involved with education in both of two ways. We have been helped in learning, that is what an educator does, and we have helped others learn. These natural human activities take place every day in all sorts of activities and few of them are organized into a formal process. When we think of "education" we usually think of schools, colleges, and universities, but as was suggested in an earlier chapter our knowledge, ideas, and beliefs are probably influenced more by the non-formal processes which we share with those around us.

Addressing the complex threats of poverty is an educational task for which most of us are not prepared. But helping us as individuals, and as a society, understand the deeper issues poverty poses is an educational task for which universities and colleges have both capacity and responsibility. They have this distinctive responsibility because professionals in many fields who have to deal with poverty as part of their work receive their preparation in university professional schools, yet only rarely is a course on poverty included in that preparation.

Before we go further in suggesting what higher education should be doing about poverty, we need to return to the observation above, that all of us are educators, and many of us are, or could be, involved in that activity in a deliberate and organized way. For that reason chapter eleven has been included as a resource for you or anyone else who chooses, or is invited, to help others realize how we take for granted a social arrangement that blights the lives of millions. To understand poverty requires a two-track approach. The common track taken since the industrial revolution has focused on the inadequacies of poor individuals and groups, and in doing so has failed to address the structures of society which constitute a more fundamental cause. That is the other track, as indicated in the title of the next chapter, which is essential to a realistic understanding of poverty. Such understanding is a critical requirement if our efforts to overcome poverty are to be effective.

What follows here is something of a prelude to the ideas and suggestions which can be employed by anyone, whether teacher, journalist, seminar leader, or preacher, who seeks to encourage others to think about poverty in a new way. The ideas and suggestions are developed in more detail in the next chapter. They begin with the need to realize that everyone has a history. How we and our students think and what we believe have been shaped by our individual histories. What we, and they, can be is influenced by what we, and they, have been. In other words we, both teachers and students, always begin in the middle.

Faculty members who try to teach a course that focuses on both personal and systemic causes of poverty, will find that resource material is very limited. Therefore a study of poverty that is committed to taking a holistic view requires a more creative approach than handing out a bibliography, assigning readings, and testing for familiarity with the literature. It calls for both teachers and students to engage in exploring their local and state situations.

Our claim that universities and colleges have the primary role in this educational task is based on the simple premise that one starts first with the teachers of teachers. Since the task is so fundamental, and confronts powerful odds, it is foolish to expect dramatic changes in a year or two. It is also unrealistic to assume that those now bearing responsibility for the welfare of such institutions can easily change gears and function on new assumptions. The pressure of time and day to day institutional operations are too great, so assuring changes requires that attention be focused on future leaders.

For this reason those preparing for leadership in the country, those who are now in the universities, need help to incorporate the issue of social and economic justice into their views of their professions. Harvard

University's School of Business developed a program to include consideration of ethics in every course. That can be a model for other universities to incorporate consideration of economic and social justice into the curricula of all professional schools. The book, *Can Ethics Be Taught?*, which describes the process by which the Harvard School of Business prepared its program, begins with describing the barriers that will be met.[27]

Any attempt to include the study of poverty in the present university curricula, or to consider poverty as a valid academic field for advanced study, will be challenged. As we have noted, resources are limited if the approach is holistic because most present studies, research, documentation, theorizing, statistics, program plans, and reports neglect the reality of systemic causes.

Other problems will stem from current lack of interest on the part of students in studying poverty, and therefore the need to require it in professional training. Even then, students approaching such study will reflect common public attitudes which include fixed views and beliefs about the poor. Therefore any course on poverty requires extensive orientation, clarifying categories, and examining views that can be tested, revised, and adapted before objective study begins.

Once the gate is opened, however, the field spreads out with numerous aspects deserving attention and challenging the understanding we may have of poverty across the world. Universities have particular responsibility to prepare leaders, whatever their fields, to share in educating the public.

Employers

Since there are so many different settings in which the poor are employed, no one approach can fit them all. We have already contended that ultimately systemic poverty can be overcome only by paying all employed poor a living wage. Advancing toward that objective can be swift for some, slow for others.

In this effort, dependence on leaders is as important as in the other sectors. Many individuals and corporations that employ the poor

148

can afford to promptly move to paying a living wage to all employees, and should do so without needing the prods of government or advocacy groups. For others, incremental steps will be necessary.

Some employers have already addressed the problem by setting a policy of the difference in pay between those at the bottom and those at the top as no more than a factor of three. Unless the head of a corporation or the Board of Directors has come to see the importance of a living wage, it is difficult for managers at lower levels to make policy changes. When the managers of three hotels in one city decided to make the wages fairer for those who clean the rooms and keep up the grounds, all three were removed by their corporate owners. And when the manager of an affluent country club raised the pay of staff who had been dependent on food stamps, he was fired. Too often corporations and their employers assume they are justified in making the minimum wage the ceiling as well as the floor for essential workers.

Historian Lawrence B. Glickman, who has given extended attention to the subject, in his 1997 book, *A Living Wage*, reports that the idea of a living wage is not new. Dating the origin of the term is difficult, but most contemporaries believe it was invented by British miners in the early 1870s. "Hugh Lloyd Jones popularized the term in a series of articles in the *Beehive*, to which those seeking the origins of the term invariably pointed. . . After the 1887 railroad strike living wage became a keyword in American labor rhetoric."[28]

B.W. Williams, in 1887, contended that for the American laborer "His earnings ought to be sufficient to enable him to live as a respectable American citizen. His living therefore must include not only food and raiment for himself and family, but also such other items as taxes, school books, furniture, newspapers, doctor bills, contributions to the cause of religion etc."[29]

Ensuing discussions have had an impact and Glickman provides this rather extended review of the present situation:

Demands for a living wage have become staple not only of national political speeches but of grass-roots movements as well. Several states and municipalities, prodded by the campaign of organized labor and activist groups, have passed "living wage" laws, which usually set a wage floor half again that of the current minimum wage. North Dakota's pioneering "Living Wage Amendment," passed in 1992, requires businesses that accept government subsidies to pay their full-time workers enough money to keep a family of four out of poverty. In 1992 it was $6.71 per hour, far exceeding the national minimum wage of $4.25. Baltimore enacted a "living wage" ordinance requiring all city contractors to pay their employees at a rate which exceeds the poverty level, $6.10 per hour as of July 1, 1995, to increase to $7.70 over the next several years. Living wage bills have also been proposed in St. Paul, Milwaukee, Houston, and New York City, where in 1995 Councilman Sal Albanese sponsored legislation to set the minimum for city contracts at twelve dollars an hour. The platform of the New Mexico Green Party calls for a "national debate" on the living wage, and the recently formed Labor Party endorses a national "living wage" of ten dollars an hour.[30]

For those who thought pay should be based on what a worker produces, "Living wage was a new concept because it was based on a consumerist view, not the just price for the product but remuneration commensurate with the needs of workers and their families. Basing remuneration on needs was a startling new idea."[31]

Thousands of individuals and institutions employing small numbers of the poor can afford to pay them a living wage now, as they do for the rest of their employees. They may say, "But we can get people for less than that so why should we pay more than the market requires?"

Employers saying that fail to realize that in doing so they are asking their employees to live in poor housing, send their children to poor schools, make them turn to charity for necessities, and cause them constant ignominy.

Raising the pay of the poor to a living wage would increase cost for employers but those costs will be passed on to consumers, as they should be. All of us now benefit from the deprivation we inflict on employed poor. To continue with the status quo is saying to them, "It is all right for you to do without so we can have what we want." We are all partners in keeping the employed poor the most unfairly treated people in our society. By taking our benefits for granted, every economic decision we make has that social consequence.

A broader and more long-range approach will need to be adopted in the relation between industries in this country and industries in other countries where very low wages are paid. A living wage should be considered as an essential part of human rights, there as well as here. United States trade negotiations should make it clear that this country will purchase goods and services only from industries that pay a living wage to all employees. The "market" would then be a positive, not just a negative, tool of social pressure. It would focus on improving the lot of those at the bottom in other countries rather than making their conditions worse.

Government

Government in this country is multiheaded. The common assumption is that "government" refers to the federal.

We have identified ways government can be a contributor to economic justice. The most immediate is its policies on wages to their essential workers. Another is to help bring equality among employers in raising the legal minimum wage to a living wage for all. When workers are paid a living wage they are no longer dependent on government or private welfare to survive. And when those government and private agencies are relieved of the millions of bottom workers who now have to turn to charity to survive those helping agencies can focus more sharply on their responsibility for the remaining poor groups:

A. those who cannot work, for many valid reasons, and

B. those who are not working, for many valid and invalid reasons. This division of the task is important and should be clarified jointly by both governmental and private agencies.

Governments are the means by which all citizens share our common responsibilities to care for the poor. That task should not be shoved over to private agencies which are dependent on the benevolent; that approach allows the non-benevolent to be freeloaders. The poor who cannot work depend on all of us. Government has primary responsibility in caring for those who cannot make it on their own.

Gulf War lingo produced a new term for talking about the terrible casualties visited on the bombed Iraqis, they were just "collateral damage." Well, social agencies are assigned to address the "collateral damage" suffered by those who, because of their genes, or behavior, or circumstances, or treatment by society, have become victims. Among them in ours, as in every society, are misfits, handicapped, disturbed, retarded, blind, senile, violent, ill, addicted people who must be helped. All of these people raise problems of health care, or better medical attention, job training, and other services, problems made much harder to solve because of recent mood changes by the public toward such people. It has become all right not to care.

Obviously "doing something" about these responsibilities rests first upon those whom we have elected to represent us in meeting common needs. This means that we should be careful about whom we elect for they must choose competent staffs to administer agencies, and professional case workers able to deal with each kind of need. Advocates, either individually or in groups, need to make sure that government representatives give attention to continuing social need even when they are preoccupied with other problems. Eternal vigilance is as essential for justice as it is for liberty.

Clergy

The problem confronts the religious communities in a very basic way. As we have seen, the regional or state judicatories of some religious organizations have adopted important statements about the ethical and moral demands of their traditions. With few exceptions, the over-whelming majority of benevolent-minded believers have accepted the common assumption that people are poor because of their inadequacies so what they need can be met by charity. A troubling question is: why do we make others beg so that we can feel benevolent? Do we expect that our religious commitments should assure us that we are superior to others? Why do we look down on those upon whom we depend?

It is strange that humans beings are reluctant to admit what benefits them may harm others; when recipients of charity make it possible for us to be virtuous while we demean them for their dependence; when we have antipathy for the employed poor who subsidize us all. We do not want to admit that humans can be as creative in injustice as in good.

Those of us who are members of religious organizations and take part in worship, educational, and service activities of our congregations, and particularly those of us who serve on congregational committees or represent the congregation on the regional or national level, have numerous opportunities to influence actions attempting to address a problem that is systemic. These opportunities include:

a) assuring that a living wage is paid to all employees of our local, state, regional, and national units;

b) engaging individuals and groups in educational programs that face squarely and honestly the consequences of neglecting to address systemic poverty;

c) encouraging pastors, rabbis, and priests to give greater emphasis to the claims of justice in their teaching and preaching; and

d) taking every possible opportunity to let the public know that religious bodies have civic responsibilities that include pressing the society at large to provide "liberty and justice for all."

There should be no illusion about accomplishing these things promptly or easily. Actually it may be more difficult for religious communities to make the needed changes than for other sectors. We have sanctified not only our beliefs and actions but also our institutions and their practices. Isaiah and Jeremiah did not have a very high regard for those who sanctify what they make.

If there is no way for reason to accompany faith, we may have made our particular definition of faith into a closed room. It then not only shuts us in but prevents us from sharing the common humanity which our religious traditions assert. When that is done it is very difficult to recognize the damaging consequences of good intentions, a Biblically recognized human failing.

The anthropologist Vernie Davis offers an analogy to our situation from more than two hundred years ago, when the Quaker leader John Woolman (d. 1772) tried to persuade his fellow Britons, who were enjoying its economic benefits, that the slave trade was evil. Davis has written:

> Woolman's approach to these issues is especially useful because it challenges the popular view that the individual is powerless to affect social change. By analyzing the structural roots of social injustice, Woolman identifies individual responsibility in a way that seeks not to point blame but to provide appropiate and meaningful ways in which the individual has the ability to respond.
>
> As John Woolman observed about people's inability to see slavery for the evil it was, the fact that the slave trade was an accepted practice that so many Christians were involved in made people less apt to examine the practice than if it were just now being proposed as a new idea. It is difficult to question something which is currently accepted, especially when it is not only accepted but appears to be in our self interest if we are to maintain our present way of life. Imagine what it would be like for 18th century plantation owners before the invention of the cotton gin to consider seriously the ethics of slave holding. The recognition that they were dependent on slave labor to maintain the life they had grown accustomed to and the recognition that slave holding was contrary to the laws of God would be impossible to hold simultaneously. . .
>
> In response to the argument that slavery protected Africans from wars in Africa and that Africans were better off as slaves, he noted that "the love of ease and gain are the motives in general of keeping slaves, and men are wont to take hold of weak arguments to support a cause which is unreasonable."[32]

Permission to quote granted by Vernie Davis.

FOR REFLECTION

The key to addressing our poverty system is recognizing that we hold two common unfair expectations of the poor: that they provide us with essential services while being paid less than it costs them to live, and that they then must seek our charity in order to survive and in doing so provide us with opportunities to be virtuous.

This arrangement is unjust. It reneges on our country's pledge to observe International Human Rights. It makes clear our failure to live by the ethical claims of our religious faiths. And it is rending the social fabric of our society.

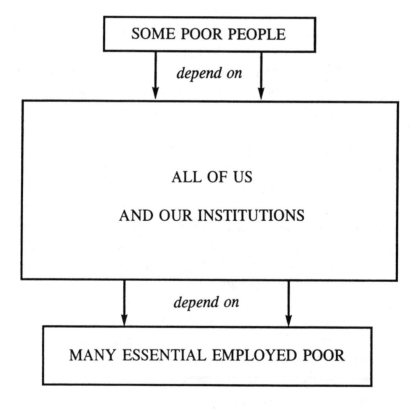

Justice: every employed person deserves a living wage.

Chapter 11

TEACHING: THE OTHER TRACK

If you have decided, or have been asked, to teach a course on poverty you will discover that it can be a fascinating and challenging task. In light of inadequacies in the way poverty is dealt with in this country, finding a more appropriate way requires a better understanding of the role and function of poverty in our society.

Most people already know about the poor and have been exposed to common attitudes and beliefs about the causes of poverty, but they may never have had an opportunity to carefully examine the validity of those beliefs and attitudes. Therefore, the objective in offering a course on poverty is to deepen and broaden the understanding of both teacher and student about this critical social reality.

The following pages are intended as a road map, not a manual spelling out the right way to conduct such a course. Possible procedures, activities, and materials are grouped under general headings or themes, recognizing that you may know of, or find, other sources to assist with particular aspects of your study.

Rationale

This country needs some way to overcome the deprivation, isolation, loss of health, and loss of talent that constitute poverty's threat to our nation's social fabric. Many public and private programs of the past three decades have provided essential help to the needy, but their efforts have been seriously handicapped because they focus on consequences, rather than on the fundamental causes, of the threat. A new perspective on the reality and dangers of deprivation and despair is required.

156

Both leaders and the public at large need to understand that poverty is perpetuated by stereotypes which misrepresent reality, by the historical role of the poor that is built into inherited institutional structures and practices, by the failure of those in power to understand the true dimensions of its blight, by the benefits it provides to the non-poor, and by its importance to the political, religious, economic, and cultural character of our society.

Providing that understanding requires confronting antipathy toward the poor, hostility toward government welfare programs, opposition to unions, policies based on simplistic assumptions as well as attitudes that people are poor because of their own inadequacies. These, too, are threats.

Addressing such complex threats is an educational task, requiring an objective arena where the problems can be studied more realistically, and future leaders prepared to resolve them. Higher education has this distinctive responsibility because professionals in many fields, who have to deal with poverty as part of their work, receive their preparation in university professional schools.

The study of poverty is usually absent from such preparation, so correcting that void is the most effective first step in helping future leaders and the public at large to understand the problems of poverty, how they are initiated and perpetuated, as well as how they may be overcome.

Problems

Among several rather obvious problems faced by anyone planning or conducting a course on poverty, the most serious problem is that both professor and students feel that they already know about poverty and have had experiences that shaped their attitudes, beliefs, and behavior about the issue. But very few have had an opportunity to examine the validity of those beliefs and attitudes.

A second serious problem in preparing for a course on poverty is the false assumption underlying this society's approach to poverty. Common interpretations of the social situation, and programs conducted to alleviate the condition, assume that poverty's basic cause is the personal inadequacies of the poor. This assumption has prevented recognition of the role of poverty in our social system. As a consequence there are now mountains of studies, research, documentation, theories, statistics, program plans, reports, records of efforts, and descriptions of poor individuals and families, all focused on one side of the subject.

This means that there is very limited resource material with which to analyze the societal functions of poverty. Therefore a study of poverty that is committed to a holistic view requires a more creative approach than handing out a bibliography, assigning readings, and then testing each student's comprehension of the literature.

The first step in preparing and conducting such a course may be that of examining one's own experience, exposure, and views about this troubling social reality. The next step can be to engage students in the same exercise. Chapter 2 offers several possible procedures for this process. They can lead to identifying tentative categories for an overall view of poverty which can be tested, revised, and adapted as the class explores the available literature, the experiences of students, the conditions of the community or region, and information provided by the media.

Terminology

As indicated in Chapter 2, terminology about the subject is a problem because the word "poverty" does not mean the same for all of us. Usually poor and poverty are used interchangeably. But "poverty" implies a structure of some kind while "poor" is always a relative word and can refer to quite different relations to society. For many Americans "poor" is synonymous with "welfare recipient."

It will be important to spend some time clarifying and defining terms so that both professor and students can talk with each other meaningfully. We can be helped in this by using the common concern in our culture about *work* to designate the meaning of "poor" in four distinguishable patterns as those who:

1. **Cannot Work.** The poor who, because of physical

handicaps or mental conditions, or age, cannot work and therefore must depend on the whole society for their care.

2. **Could Work.** The poor who are not working outside the home because of family responsibilities, restricted backgrounds, limited education, and other handicaps, but could work if provided with appropriate help.

3. **Are Self-Employed.** Many poor are working as plumbers, poets, midwives, farmers, or fishermen and want to be on their own. They may occasionally need assistance but are not part of the welfare system.

4. **Are Employed by Others.** Different from the other patterns, but including many more people than all of the others. They are poor men and women, and their households, who are caught in the poverty system in which essential workers are paid less than it costs them to live.

Combining patterns 3 and 4 in studies or statistics as "the working poor" misrepresents and confuses the understanding of systemic poverty. In order for careful study as for discussion in class or seminar to be realistic, clarifying the meanings of "poor" needs to be accompanied by recognizing that the word "poverty" is used in two very different ways:

A. When poverty refers to conditions under which individuals and families live, diagnosing its cause(s) can be specific and ways to overcome their condition can be direct and obvious.

B. However, when poverty refers to an aspect of a socio-economic system which requires that some people be poor, diagnosing its causes involves a very different arena, and overcoming those causes is a much more complex task.

Care in using the words correctly can be preparation for the "creative approach" to studying poverty referred to above, and this involves direct involvement with the world of the poor.

Examining the System

There is no body of standard works to which students can be sent for an introduction to and a description of a system in which the employed poor are essential to the maintenance of all organizations and institutions. This limitation offers opportunities to make the study of poverty more interesting and challenging to students because they can do their own research.

Evidence of the system is available in every community in the country. There is no need to search for authorities who provide data. In fact, the objective of this course is to broaden each student's understanding of poverty, and statistics are of little help with that challenge. Cause has to do with structure, ideas, beliefs, values and attitudes.

Every day all of us are served by people whose income is below what it costs them to live. They are the essential employed poor on whom we all depend. Studying how the system needs them and yet pays them poorly is a close-at-hand opportunity for examining the system and its consequences.

Here are several illustrations of that opportunity, but first some consideration should be given to general guidelines that can increase the value of such experiences.

a) When an individual student is acting alone to observe or collect points of view, five to ten illustrations will provide a better basis for generalization than one or two.

b) If students choose to do interviews, it is wise to do so in pairs. This does not overwhelm the person being interviewed, but each can give assistance to the other in the process, and it enables them to confer about what they have done.

c) The activities of individual students and pairs of students to learn about the poverty system first-hand needs to be shared with the whole class. This can be done in a variety of ways such as: written report, posing issues to class members, dividing the class into two or three groups with each considering insights and then sharing or comparing insights with the other group, or a display, or a dramatic presentation.

160

1. *Being served.* In order to become more aware of the many who serve us, both directly and indirectly making one's own list and noting them day by day for a week may indicate the extent of our dependence on them.

2. *Jobs.* Examine the "Help Wanted" ads in the local paper and check out ten to find out about hours, pay, benefits, job security, what is expected of an employee, where you would have to live, transportation costs, attire, and under whom you would have to work.

3. *Go there.* Visit in the poor side of the city or town. Go to places where you could get acquainted with a resident and explain that you want help in understanding the community and how people get along. You might meet with small groups, walk the streets, and watch children play. Let someone there be your teacher so you can understand something about what it means to live among the poor.

4. *Big institutions.* If you live or are studying in a city or location where large corporations have plants and offices, do a survey of the number of "bottom jobs" required in a bank, club, architect's office, medical office, or manufacturing plant and, if possible, find out what the employment policies are. It could be important to keep notes on the reactions and attitudes of those from whom you would like to obtain information. What do the results say to you?

5. *In the news.* Read the daily paper for two weeks and clip every item about the poor. Put them together in a notebook. At the end of the two weeks, group the clippings according to themes (about jobs, welfare, personal experiences, causes of being poor, legal action, etc.) and do a one-page summary of the principal insights. Even better, have a partner do the same thing and see how you agree or differ in your interpretation of what you have read.

6. *Who helps?* Select three social agencies in your community that serve the poor and make an appointment to go with another student to find out the kind of service provided, the kinds of clients being served, and the proportion of clients who are employed but need help beyond what they earn. Compare the results with the experiences of other students who visit other agencies.

7. *Attitudes and beliefs.* Interview clergy people or church staff

members to find out the proportion of the congregation who are employed poor, why there is that proportion, the pay scale of church employees, and whether the church has a charity program for the poor. Interview church members and discuss their attitudes and beliefs about the poverty situation in the community.

Causes

The following books provide a range of interpretations of the causes of poverty.

The Poverty Establishment, ed. Pamela A. Roby (Paramus, NJ: Prentice-Hall, 1974)

Section 5. Causes of Poverty

The Economics of Poverty and Discrimination, by Bradley R. Schiller (Paramus, NJ: Prentice-Hall, 1984)

Part 2. The Causes of Poverty

Living Poorly in America, by Leonard Beeghley (New York: Praeger, 1983)

Chapter 7. The Causes of Poverty

This chapter begins by noting the contrast between inquiring into why people are poor from inquiring why social processes produce impoverished persons.

Cultural Values

Considering poverty as primarily an economic matter fails to recognize that economic patterns depend upon common agreements (assumptions, beliefs, attitudes, ideas) that enable the society to function in a certain way. The persistence of poverty is a direct product of accepted and taken-for-granted social patterns. Therefore, understanding poverty involves understanding the various values which are held as central to those ideas, attitudes, beliefs, and assumptions. In their 1988 book on *Dependency and Poverty, Old Problems in a New World* (Lexington, MA: Lexington Books, 1988) June Axinn and Mark Stern examine many different ways in which the poor are dependent on the government and

162

society but they give no consideration to how society is dependent on underpaid employees.

Books about American culture abound and the attributes most frequently identified as characteristics of this society are work, competition, individualism, private ownership, and freedom. The way these attributes affect the social structure, and particularly those working at low-status jobs, is examined by many writers, the four indicated here being rather typical.

The Forgotten Americans, by John E. Schwarz and Thomas J. Volgy (New York: W.W. Norton, 1992)

Chapter 1. The American Ethos and the American People

Chapter 2. Working Americans and Economic Hardship

The Poverty Establishment, ed. Pamela A. Roby (Paramus, NJ: Prentice-Hall, 1974)

Section 1. How the establishment keeps the poor poor and the rich rich.

Middle American Individualism, the Future of Liberal Democracy, by Herbert J. Gans (New York: The Free Press, 1988)

See especially pages 4f, 108f, and 135

Social Darwinism in American Thought, by Richard Hofstadter (Boston: Beacon Press, 1955)

In dealing with various aspects of American culture Hofstadter gives extensive accounts of the American commitment to competition and individualism.

Dealing with Poverty

The persistence of poverty is also rooted in public and private efforts to ameliorate or overcome poverty. Most of the studies about dealing with poverty have focused on governmental policies and programs. For many scholars "overcoming poverty" means receiving an *income plus charity* that totals more than the federal poverty line. But there is now increasing awareness that getting out of poverty means having a household income twice the poverty line.

Historically it has been unions, to improve life for their members, that have mounted the most effective efforts to overcome the poverty system. The low regard with which many now view unions in this country suggests that most people have had no opportunity to know their history or to understand what they do. These books may help correct that situation:

Labor's Untold Story, by Richard O. Boyer (Pittsburgh: UNITE, 1976)
   A history of the Labor movement in the United States

What Do Unions Do?, by Richard B. Freeman and James L. Medoff (New York: Basic Books, 1984)
   An overview of accomplishments and problems of unions.

Unions and Economic Competitiveness, eds. Lawrence Mishel and Paula B. Voos (Armonk, NY: 1992)
   Particularly a section of Part II, on Work Organizations, Unions, and Economic Performance, by Ray Marshall

Examining the kinds of approaches described in these and other books raises the valid question that needs to be considered if the inadequacies of such approaches are to be understood: Why, in spite of the numerous public and private programs that are maintained by hundreds of thousands of able and committed people and cost billions of dollars each year, does poverty persist?

Poverty and Power, The Political Representation of Poor Americans, by Douglas R. Imig (Lincoln, Nebr: University of Nebraska Press, 1996)
   Chapters 3. Historical Development of Poverty Advocacy, and
      6. Political Opportunities and Antipoverty Activism

   To indicate the range of that aadvocacy and activism Professor Imig lists national organizations established between 1965 and 1981:

      Center on Social Welfare Policy and Law
      Center for Community Change
      National Association for the Southern Poor
      Children's Foundation
      Community for Creative Non-Violence
      Community Nutrition Institute
      Food Research and Action Center
      Partnership for Democracy

Children's Defense Fund
Bread for the World
Interreligion Task Force on U.S. Food Policy
Working Group on Domestic Hunger and Poverty
National Low Income Housing Coalition
Center on Budget and Policy Priorities

Attempting to gain an inclusive view of efforts to help the poor must include an examination of the major public and private agencies:

Public Agencies:

There are many sources of information in every state. The temptation of those providing information is to focus on statistics which are seldom of help in understanding situations, procedures, attitudes, and beliefs about poverty. Those who conduct the numerous programs are of more help because they can illustrate the process as they explain how they work, their evaluation of their jobs, their relation to other agencies, and their reasons for doing what they do.

State and County Departments of Social Services
State and County Departments of Public Health
Legal Services
Housing Commissions
Economic Development Agencies
Commission on Employment Security
Social Security Administration

Private Agencies:

There are numerous agencies in every county and state that provide a wide variety of services. Some groups are devoted to advocacy and have specific objectives that shape their attitudes toward clients. It is important to find out the extent to which leaders in these agencies realize the relation of charity to the system which perpetuates poverty.

Community Agencies
Fraternal Organizations
Religious Agencies
Unions
Volunteer Groups
Food Banks

Being Poor

Being poor involves living in a mainly resistent, even antagonistic, society. That resistance and antagonism has been studied and explored by many conscientious and concerned people. Two of them are Herbert J. Gans and James Graham. Neither author focuses on the employed poor, who are central to the concerns of this study, but both authors identify facets of the situation of the poor that apply to the employed poor as well. Graham's writing grows from his experiences as a lawyer who worked with settlement houses while he taught in both New York and Arizona. In his book *The Enemies of the Poor* (New York: Random House, 1970) he describes in detail why he considers lawyers, churches, unions, and community agencies as control groups that are enemies of the poor.

Other helpful writers are:

Poverty in America, by Milton Melzer (New York: William Morrow, 1986)

   Meltzer deals plainly, chapter by chapter, with
   Breadlines and Soup Kitchens
   Living in the Street
   Growing Up Poor
   Women in the Job Ghetto
   How the Elderly Live
   When a Farm Dies
   The Price of Racism
   The Dream of Abundance
   A Safety Net---with Big Holes

Growing Up Poor, by Terry M. Williams and William Kornblum (Lexington, MA: Lexington Books, 1985)

   Documents the life experiences of teenagers in specific communities in New York City, Louisville, Kentucky, Cleveland, Ohio, and Meridian, Mississippi.

The War Against the Poor, The Underclass and Antipoverty Policy, by Herbert J. Gans (New York: Basic Books, 1995)

   Gans points out that when the Swedish writer Gunnar Myrdal used the term "underclass" he used it as an economic category, but now in this country the term is being used to indicate the behavior of the poor which makes them undeserving.

Historical Roots

Having examined many aspects of the way our society views and deals with poverty, it is important to review our cultural and religious history in order to understand the depth of the roots that influence our assumptions and commitments and recognize how they contribute to the perpetuation of systemic poverty. Noted chapters in these books offer insights for consideration.

Slavery, From the Rise of Western Civilization to the Renaissance, by Milton Meltzer (New York: Cowles Book Co., 1971)

 1. Thing or Person
 3. In the Valley of the Nile
 6. The Greek World Expands
 11. The Rise of Rome
 23. The Medieval Slave

A Social History of England, by Asa Briggs (New York, Viking, 1984)

 8. The Experience of Industrialization

Issues in American Economic History; Selected Readings, ed. Gerald D. Nash (Lexington, MA: D.C. Heath, 1992)

 32. American Economic Expansion and the American Character

Although a basic course on poverty cannot include an exploration of the long history of religious involvement, two current aspects can be illuminated by looking at the past:

a) the relation of religious communities to governments in dealing with poverty, and

b) the relation of religious views to patterns and structures of the general culture. These books can be helpful.

The Religious Factor; A Sociological Study of Religion's Impact on Politics, Economics, and Family Life, by Gerhard Lenski (New York: Doubleday, 1963)

 3. Religion and Economics

4. Religion and Politics

8. Conclusions

The Protestant Establishment; Aristocracy & Caste in America, by E.
Digby Baltzell (New York: Vintage Books, 1966)

3. The Immigrant's Progress and the Theory of the Establishment

4. The Ideological Defense of Caste

11. The Intellectuals Abandon the Caste Establishment

14. Caste and Corporations

15. Aristocracy on the Campus

The English Poor Law 1780-1930, Michael E. Rose, Comp. (Newton
Abbot, England: David & Charles, 1971)

The Poor Law was passed under Queen Elizabeth in 1601, placing
responsibilities for the poor upon local parishes.

Professional Issues

Certain professions involve responsibilities for dealing directly with the
poor and poverty issues on both individual and institutional levels.
Fulfilling those responsibilities varies from profession to profession as do
the specific issues they confront. The following indicates some of those
issues in eight professional fields:

The Arts, including movies, fiction, photography, painting

Issues such as:

The "picture" of the poor that is settled in the minds of the public

The influence of movies and popular television shows on how people
think about the poor

How can one "picture" the system?

Escaping common stereotypes in drama, poetry, novels

Eliminating romanticizing the poor who work on their own

Care in relating poverty to race or ethnicity

obtain reliable information

How the poor "picture" themselves when they are

(1) unable to work

(2) looking for a job

(3) self-employed

(4) employed with an income less than a living wage

and/or

Business

Issues such as:

The extent to which Adam Smith's ideas about society actually shape economic decisions here and now

Other forces such as technology and globalization that may be more influential in the economy of the United States than in other countries

The ethical justification for paying essential workers less than it costs them to live, both in the United States and in other countries

How to relate the pressure for profits to one's family situation

Squaring the claims of the company, organization, or institution, with personal convictions and beliefs

Principles that should guide relationships with those above and below us in the hierarchy of institutions with which we are involved

How paying a living wage to workers relieves the burden on welfare and taxes, and can benefit the local economy

and/or

Education

Issues such as:

The distinction between public education and education of the public

Ethical aspects for educators to consider as they deal with problems of poverty

Gaining self-understanding about one's own attitudes toward the poor

Ways professors and teachers who are from the non-poor world can gain a realistic understanding of the world of the poor

Ways one's understanding of the poor influences one's relation to the poor

Responsibility for preparing students to expand their exposure to what is happening in the world

Clarifying multiple academic responsibilities: professor to institution, scholar to subject, and teacher to students

and/or

Journalism

Issues such as:

Responsibility to the public for honest reporting of facts and situations

Resisting the clout of the powerful to shape the interpretation of events

Resisting the pressure of time that can prevent full knowledge of matters toward which many in the public have antipathy or judge unfairly

Relating one's own upbringing and social experiences to the situations of people being interviewed or reported on, particularly when they are of the poor world

Recognizing the influence of one's own ideology and beliefs upon the fairness of one's reporting or being a columnist

Securing a functional defense against lobbying pressures to make the news beneficial to particular individuals or institutions

Responsibility of the news media to educate/inform the public about the ways the poverty system works

and/or

Law

Issues such as:

Whether dependence on pro bono services provides equal justice under the law

The role of the powerless in establishing equality under the law

Clarifying the differences in claims for justice between individuals and institutions in this pluralistic society

Distinguishing between protection of an affluent client and one's social responsibility for the welfare of the poor

Relating one's own social encounters to seeing the impact of the system on those who have no access to power

and/or

Medicine

Issues such as:

Keeping up with the numerous studies on the effects of poverty on health

170

The implications of what is learned from those studies for working
with individual poor people

Responsibilities for policies and positions taken by professional
groups to which one belongs

Obligations of specialists to public health efforts

Ethical implications of medical professions' stance on developing a
system to provide basic health care to everyone

How the living conditions of patients should influence the physician's
diagnosis and recommendations for treatment

How health research and administration relate to patient's life condition
and/or

Politics

Issues such as:

Since one obvious characteristic of the poor is their powerlessness,
what operating influences can maintain consideration of legal rights
and public programs for the poor

How to determine the appropriate responsibilities for each of the
various levels of government in dealing with the poverty system

What political function is appropriate for the poor

Considering the relative influence of advocacy groups for the poor in
attaining a fair and just society

The impact of international agreements about human rights upon the
lawmaking at various governmental levels
and/or

Religion

Issues such as:

Different views of poverty and the cultural ground from which they
grow in the world religions that are increasing in this country

The public and civic responsibility of religious organizations

Ways religious communities can resist the influence of wealthy donors
who prefer to stress charity rather than a living wage for employees

Problems of maintaining "freedom of the pulpit" when considering
economic and political issues

Relating the commitment to justice in different religious traditions to the immediate issues of justice at the local, state, and national levels

Understanding the possible strengths of congregations as change agents in efforts to change systemic poverty

* * * * *

FOR REFLECTION

From *The Idea of Poverty, England in the Early Industrial Age,* by Gertrude Himmelfarb

Pages 3, 4

It says a good deal about the history of modern England that the eighteenth century Tory and the twentieth century Socialist should agree about this if about little else, that the condition of the poor is the "touchstone" of a civilization, a nation, a philosophy. They disagreed, to be sure, about what constituted a "decent provision" for the poor, a disagreement that reflected not only the ideological differences between Tory and Socialist but a century and a half of economic, technological, social, and cultural changes which profoundly transformed the very idea of poverty as much as the condition of the poor. Yet it is surely significant that on the eve of that transformation, from the heart of that "old society," there should have issued sentiments which could so readily have been endorsed by one of the most progressive thinkers of our own time. Whatever else changed during this period, in this respect at least the end was in the beginning.

The "beginning" can, of course, be taken back to the very beginning when it was first discovered that "ye have the poor always with you." That thought came echoing down through the centuries with the authority of Scripture and the practical wisdom of the ages. And with it came a complicated (ambivalent, we would now think of it) conception of pov-

172

erty, which made it at the same time a blessing to be devoutly sought and a misfortune to be piously endured. The "holy poor" embraced poverty as a sacred vow, the better to do God's will; the "unholy poor" tolerated it (or railed against it) as an unhappy fact of life, a cross to be borne with Christian fortitude or resisted with unChristian defiance. Those who were blessed not with poverty but with riches had the sacred duty of charity, the obligation to sustain the holy poor and to relieve the misery of the unholy. With every aspect of poverty and charity penetrated by religious meaning, the church inevitably became the instrument both of social amelioration and of spiritual salvation; indeed the one was a function of the other.

By Samuel Johnson's time, the conception of poverty had become largely secularized, so that it came to mean, in common usage, the involuntary, ignoble poverty of the "lower orders." This is not to say that there was anything impious in this conception. Johnson himself, a man of the firmest religious convictions, had no doubt that poverty had its source and justification in the primeval Fall, which condemned man to toil all the days of his life and to eat his bread by the sweat of his brow. But neither had he any romantic illusions about the ennobling nature of that poverty.

Pages 7, 8

One of the mediating facts that intervened between problem and solution and played a crucial part in this history was the set of ideas contemporaries brought to it, ideas about how to mitigate or "solve" the problem of poverty, and ideas about what constituted poverty and what made it a problem requiring remedy or solution. This raises a host of questions that are somewhat different from the conventional concerns of the social historian. What was the idea or conception of poverty that elevated it to the status of a problem? How did one conception give way to another, so that the "natural," unproblematic poverty of one age became the urgent social problem of another? Which of the poor were regarded as problematic, and how did the popular image of that group affect the proposals for reform? How were the "unworthy," "undeserving" poor distinguished from the "worthy" and "deserving," and why was it that first the former and then the latter became the primary focus of the social problem? How did the concept of the "deserving poor" become redefined so as to make them eligible for public assistance, when earlier they were thought deserving precisely because they were self-sustaining, hence not in need of assistance? How did the largely undifferentiated poor of earlier times ("the poor "equated with the "lower orders") become highly differentiated, the "dependent" poor being sharply distinguished from the "independent," the "pauper" from the "laboring poor," the "residuum" from the "respectable poor"? How were essentially moral categories integrated with the later "objective" definitions of poverty based on income and subsistence? And how did conceptions, definitions, and categories relate to the prevailing social ethos, the moral and intellectual climate that affected the condition of the poor as well as the disposition of those reformers who took it upon themselves to improve that condition?

None of these questions can be divorced from the familiar issues of "problems" and "solutions." Yet they are a different order of questions and require a different treatment. Even when they draw upon the same materials for their answers, they use those materials in a different way, eliciting from them different kinds of information and meanings. To ask these questions, to address oneself to the "idea" of poverty in this sense, is not to belittle either the problem of poverty or the policies designed to ameliorate it. It is rather an effort to elucidate both by adding another dimension to the social reality.

Pages 10, 11

The "idea of poverty" is obviously a hybrid subject, a cross between two distinct species, social history and intellectual history. If the social historian finds the "idea" in the title obtrusive, an unnecessary complication and distraction from the "real" subject of poverty, the intellectual historian may object to an "idea" that is vague and amorphous, more often implicit than explicit, not at all the respectable kind of idea he is accustomed to. It is not an idea which lends itself to rigorous philosophical analysis. Nor can it be found in philosophical texts; there were, in fact, no treatises on "the idea of poverty." Nor, for that matter, have there been any histories of the subject (on the order, for example, of histories on the idea of progress). Embedded in the social milieu, the idea can only be extracted from that milieu, from the behavior of people as well as from their writings, from legislation and debates, popular movements and public issues, economic treatises and religious tracts, novels, and "penny dreadfuls." "Idea" in this sense is a shorthand expression for a complex of concepts, attitude, values, beliefs, perceptions, images.

Pages 18, 19

In this sense, 1760, the somewhat arbitrary date assigned to the somewhat hyperbolic event known as the industrial revolution, marked a decisive turning point. For it was then that poverty was removed from nature and brought into the forefront of history. That had happened on occasion before, when the decline of feudalism "liberated" the poor and threw them upon the mercies, not of a free economy but of a freer one; or when the enclosure movement of the sixteenth century disrupted age-old conventions of land tenure and created new conditions, and opportunities, of life and work; or, on a smaller scale, at all times and places when social changes loomed larger for contemporaries than they do in historical retrospect. On each of these occasions the new condition was soon assimilated into the old, made to seem eminently natural, yet another variation on the eternal phenomenon of the poor who are "always with you."

After the middle of the eighteenth century it became increasingly difficult to take refuge in that timeless maxim. If the poor were as omnipresent as ever, indeed, more plentiful than ever, given the rapid increase of population and thus the vastly increased numbers of poor, they were also more problematic than ever. All the changes coming to a head at this time, technological, economic, demographic, political, ideological, affected the poor to a greater degree than any other class and made their poverty more conspicuous, more controversial, and in a sense less natural" than it had ever been before. And this in spite of notable attempts to "naturalize" poverty, to subject it, as Adam Smith did, to the natural laws of political economy, or, as Malthus did, to the biological laws of food and sex. Malthus complained that previous histories had been exclusively histories of the "higher classes," that they had ignored that large part of mankind, the poor, who had borne the brunt of the pressure of population and food. After Malthus, no one could make that complaint. The poor, if they were not the subject of written histories, were visibly, consciously the subject of history itself.

It was thus that the "annals of the poor" ceased to be "short and simple" and became long and complicated. In the period of only a century, circumstances conspired to create a highly differentiated poor, with different groups, at different times, in different conditions, with different characteristics, emerging as "the social problem." This was not a matter, as a later generation was to think, of raising or lowering the "poverty level" so that more or fewer of the poor were included in that rubric. The changes affecting the poor were changes in kind as well as degree, in quality as well as quantity, in ideas, attitudes, beliefs, perceptions, values. They were changes in what may be called the "moral imagination," the imagination that makes sense of reality, not by being imposed on reality (as ideology is) but by so thoroughly penetrating it that the reality has no form or shape apart from it.

Published New York: by Knopf, 1984. Copyright (c) by Gertrude Himmelfarb. Permission to quote granted.

Aspects of Poverty for Further Study

This chapter has offered ideas and resources for use by anyone planning a basic course on poverty. The field deserves much deeper and wider study if its full ramifications are to be appreciated or addressed, and those studies can concentrate on at least six important areas:

Sectors. There are many dimensions to be examined for poverty issues involved with each of the four power sectors of society.

Social issues. Much more work needs to done in bringing together studies presently available as well as expanding research on race, gender, crime, drugs, and their relation to educational resources.

Personal impacts involved are despair, violence, depression, resentment, cynicism, and desperation as people struggle to deal with the consequences of poverty.

Social policy is a major concern in clarifying the appropriate relation of public with private approaches for helping the victims of poverty.

Geography poses broad problems in relating the special attention given to the shifting differences between urban and rural poverty.

World poverty. The United Nations, World Watch, and the Inter-American Development Bank are but three of many organizations that are continuing to study, report on, and attempt to address the differing issues in Asia, Africa, Europe, Central and South America. Special attention needs to be given to perpetuation of poverty in countries where workers are paid low wages by American employers.

ENDNOTES

1. Excerpted from *19 Reasons for Being in Poverty* (Greensboro, NC: Human Services Institute, 1986). Drawings by Tim Rickard.

2. Jacqueline Jones, *The Dispossessed* (New York: Basic Books, 1992), p. 35.

3. Jonathan Kozol, *Savage Inequalities: Children in America's Schools* (New York: Crown Publishers, 1991).

4. Mechal Lerner, *Surplus Powerlessness* (Oakland, CA: Institute on Labor and Mental Health, 1986), p. 2.

5. Ibid., p. 13f.

6. June Axinn and Mark Stern, *Dependency and Poverty: Old Problems in a New World* (Lexington, MA: Lexington Books, 1988).

7. Kevin Phillips, *The Politics of Rich and Poor: Wealth and the American Electorate in the Reagan Aftermath* (New York: Random House, 1990), p. 41.

8. Hastings Rashdall, *The Universities of Europe in the Middle Ages*. Vol. I. (Oxford, University Press, [1895] 1936), p. 7.

9. Ibid.

10. Ibid., p. 394.

11. Ibid., p. 428

12. Lionel S. Lewis, *Scaling the Ivory Tower: Merit and Its Limits in Academic Careers* (Baltimore: Johns Hopkins University Press, 1975)

178

13. Gene F. Summers, Andre D. Hammonds and Mary J. Miron, *Rural Poverty, A Teaching Guide and Source Book* (Boseman, MT: Rural Sociological Association, Montana State University, 1993).

14. Lawrence B. Glickman, *A Living Wage: American Workers and the Making of Consumer Society* (Ithaca, NY: Cornell University Press, 1997), p. 13.

15. Wendell Gordon and John Adams, *Economics as Social Science: An Evolutionary Approach* (Riverdale, NJ: The Riverdale Company, 1989), p. 123.

16. Ibid.

17. Bradley R. Schiller, *The Economics of Poverty and Discrimination* (Paramus, NJ: Prentice Hall, 1984), p. 66.

18. Keith Melville and Bill Carr, *The Poverty Puzzle: What Should Be Done to Help the Poor?* (Dubuque, IA: Kendall/Hunt, 1993), p. 3.

19. Ibid., p. 19.

20. Michael Harrington, *The Other America: Poverty in the United States* (New York: Macmillan, 1962).

21. Peter Meyer, "A Brief History" in *The International Bill of Human Rights*, ed. Paul Williams (Glen Ellen, NY: Entwhistle Books, 1981), p. xlii.

22. Robert McAfee Brown and Sydney Thomson Brown, eds. *A Cry for Justice: The Churches and Synagogues Speak* (New York: Paulist Press, 1989), p. 91.

23. Michael E. Rose, *The English Poor Law, 1789-1930* (New York: Barnes and Noble, 1971), p. 11.

24. Charles A. Summers, "Discipleship in the Eighties; Charity vs Justice," *Presbyterian Outlook* (September 28, 1981), pp. 5f.

25. Ivan Illich, "The Seamy Side of Charity," *America* (January 21, 1967), p. 88.

26. Paul Tillich, *Theology and Culture* (New York: Oxford University Press, 1959), p. 40.

27. Thomas R. Piper, Mary C. Gentile, and Sharon Daloz Parks, *Can Ethics Be Taught? Perspectives, Challenges, and Approaches at Harvard Business School* (Boston, MA: Harvard Business School, 1993).

28. Glickman, op cit., p. 66.

29. Ibid., p. 82.

30. Ibid., p. xii.

31. Ibid., p. 68.

32. Vernie Davis, "John Woolman and Structural Violence: Model for Analysis and Social Change." (Unpublished Paper, 1998), pp. 1, 6.

INDEX

Newton, Isaac, 105-106
North Carolina Poverty Project,
32, 33, 57-63

P

Paulsen, Frederick, 80
pay scales, 95
Pelikan, Jerislav, 74
Phillips, Kevin, 51, 99
poor, 32-36
    patterns, 157-158
    undeserving, 66
poverty, 32-36
    jobs, 26-27
    line, 16
    systemic, 21, 39
powerlessness, 44
professions, 167-170
    preparation for, 77-78

R

Rashdall, Hastings, 72-73
Reformation, 78
Reich, Robert, 101
religions, 127-142
religious rhetoric, 128
Rifkin, Jeremy, 98-101
rights, 116
    human, 117-120
    property, 116-118
    Universal Bill, 117-120
Rose, Michael, 131-132, 167

Rubin, Amy Migaro, 86
Rural Sociological Society, 76

S

Saffo, Paul, 99
sectors, 24-26
Schiller, Bradley, 94
slavery, 153
Smith, Adam, 93, 107-108, 168
social arrangement, 22, 41
stereotypes, 53-54
Stern, Mark, 47
studium generale, 72
Summers, Charles A., 134

T

temporary workers, 92
terminology, 15
Thrifty Food Plan, 18
Tillich, Paul, 137
Turner, Francis J., 85

U

universities, 70-88
    as employer, 78, 147
    Bologna, 72-73
    Cologne, 79
    Dublin, 82
    Edinburgh, 81-82
    Erfurt, 79
    Freiburg, 79

Harvard, 85, 147
Heidelburg, 79
Paris, 73
Prague, 79
Oxford, 81
Vienna, 79
Salerno, 73
Yale, 78, 86-88

V

Voos, Paula B., 163

W

War on Poverty, 49, 50, 52
welfare, 19, 114
Williams, B.W., 148
Wilson, John Oliver, 130
Wilson, Terry, 165
Woolman, John, 153
work, 25, 37-38

AFTERWORDS

The gestation period of this book has been twelve years. It is the outgrowth of unplanned exposures and discoveries that educated me. The most significant was the appearance in the local newspaper, in September of 1985, of a week-long series about North Carolina's poor. A few of us were a committee set up to study poverty in our county, but the newspaper series made it clear that we should be working on a broader basis. We decided that some prominent leaders of the state should be invited to consider what could be done about the state-wide blight.

Governor James Hunt suggested that Dr. William C. Friday, the just-retired head of the state University system, be asked to chair such an exploratory meeting. Dr. Friday was immediately interested, identified leaders to be invited, and chaired the meeting in May of 1986. The views of the group became a booklet, "Poverty and Civic Responsibility" and the concerns of the group led to the organization of the North Carolina Poverty Project, with Dr. Friday as chair of its Board of Directors for its first two years. His position as a leader in the state, his contacts, his creative ideas, and his assistance in fund raising were crucial in helping the Project establish an effective working base. The Project was a four-year commitment to help the public understand both the poverty situation in the state and what was being done about it.

I have been the volunteer Executive Director of the Poverty Project since its incorporation in January of 1987 as an "educational program on poverty and civic responsibility." During those four years we worked with all agencies serving the poor: Legal Services, Community Action, Food Banks, housing networks, county Departments of Social Services, church service ministries, etc.

With the help of staff members in those agencies we prepared a dozen booklets, such as: "How We Feed the Poor in North Carolina," "Superintendents Discuss Impact of Poverty on Public Schools," "Helping Students Study Poverty," "Community Action in North

Carolina" (a 25th anniversary issue with detailed information about each of the 43 agencies), "The Other North Carolina" (in cooperation with the Rural Economic Development Center), and "Poverty in the East" (about the poorest section of the state).

With a local television station we produced ten "public service announcements" on "Rumors and Facts about Poverty" which were aired by stations across the state.

"Open to the World" was a two-year program bringing all of the freshmen from the two high schools of a very poor county, 45 at a time, to visit the major medical centers in the state, exposing them to totally new experiences.

We conducted many conferences and consultations. One was on children and families in poverty. It brought together 75 representatives of 55 agencies, meeting one week to identify major issues and again a week later for exchange of ideas and planning. Another conference was with North Carolina Writers who then prepared a series of poems, essays, and stories that appeared in many of the state's newspapers. They also collected their writings about poverty in a booklet, "I Have Walked."

A major shift came in 1990 when a group of agency leaders urged the Poverty Project to continue, but with a change of focus. They said, "All of us are dealing with the consequences of poverty, no one with its causes. That is what you should do." The Board of Directors considered the request and decided to go into what was a new beginning and a new direction, not knowing where it might lead.

One helpful contact led to MacArthur Foundation funding of a regional exploration of the possibility of replicating the Project in the southeastern states that had the highest proportion of children in poverty in the country. The exploration was conducted over two years with interested participants from seven states sharing in a series of week-end workshops. They finally issued a major document, "The Causes of Poverty." A Poverty Project was established in Alabama, an Institute on Poverty and Deprivation in South Carolina became a Poverty Project, and the Carter Center in Atlanta joined with North Carolina in forming the Coalition Addressing Systemic Poverty.

Another major development, an outgrowth from the workshops, was prompted by the discovery that poverty was almost totally absent from the curricula of universities in our states. A workshop held in Auburn, Alabama, spelled out the elements that should be included in a basic course on poverty. We realized that to get colleges and universities to offer the study of poverty to its students a demonstration would be needed.

The Coalition developed a Program on Understanding Poverty designed particularly for students preparing to be professionals who will, during their careers, have many occasions that involve the poor and poverty issues, an inevitable experience for doctors, clergy, teachers, lawyers, politicians, journalists, and business managers. Four universities, in each of the three states, selected two professors in those fields to offer demonstration or experimental courses, using RESOURCES, a handbook prepared by the Coalition, and then to evaluate what they have done and thus assist other colleges or universities considering the inclusion of such study in their curricula.

Sharing in the initiation of these activities on both the state and regional level has required pausing, from time to time, to check on the validity and effectiveness of the efforts. Writing this book has provided such an occasion for review, but the reflection has gone beyond my involvement with poverty and the agencies devoted to serving the poor. It has become clear that the pressure of responsibility placed on those who lead and/or control the major influential institutions of our society offers them scant opportunity to consider the changes necessary if the poverty system is to be overcome. That realization has prompted a strategy of focusing on those who are now being prepared for leadership in the decades ahead. In other words, social change requires a change in the education of its leaders.

For some people "education" is a matter of training, for others it refers to a process of indoctrination, both making important contributions to society. However, on a deeper level education is a process of helping understanding, a process of help provided by many different kinds of agents: other people, social exposures, accidental encounters, institutional practices, as well as all the commercials trying to sell us things. The

188

influences that shape us are those we adopt, in other words we control what is learned.

Only later did I come to realize the general import of what I had written in my doctoral dissertation, "Revelation and Education." In its theological context revelation usually refers to sacred texts, prophetic assertions, or divine proclamations. But religious history provides numerous troubling examples of conflict among disciples over what those texts, assertions, or proclamations mean. Revelation, thus, is not what is given but what is appropriated.

John Dewey confirms this insight in his contention that "experience" is not what happens but is the interpretation of the happening, and Edmund Husserl holds the parellel view that the "phenomenon" of his phenomenology refers to the meaning we give to events and ideas. From his views comes the realization that each of us constitutes a "world" which directs our interpretations, our beliefs, and our actions.

Staff positions I have held since graduation from Union Seminary in New York have repeatedly confirmed this view of education. The first was as associate pastor of a prominent church on Park Avenue in New York, then directing young adult programs for the national Board of Education of the United Methodist Church. This led to becoming Minister of Education at two very large churches: Hennepin Avenue United Methodist Church in Minneapolis with 4,500 members (before my doctoral studies) and the Riverside Church in New York with 3,500 members (after the doctoral studies). These were followed by nineteeen years as a Professor of Education at the Pittsburgh Theological Seminary.

All of these positions provided opportunities to observe the educational impact of institutional practices. This means of educating was addressed by several members of the Philosophy of Education Society in a book, *Culture as Education*, which illustrated the educating impact of participation in the common activities of community and institutional life. The book was edited by Vincent Crockenberg and Richard LaBrecque, and published by Kendall/Hunt, Dubuque, Iowa, in 1977, and my chapter was "Churches Also Teach Unintentionally," suggesting that what institutions teach unintentionally frequently conflicts directly with what they teach intentionally.

Another perspective on that reality was illustrated when I was invited to be a consultant for the educational program of a seminary, the Facultad Evangelica de Teologia, in Buenos Aires, Argentina. The assumption was that my attention would be given to education courses, but that changed in response to what faculty members were telling me, that students who came from all parts of the country had no idea of what it was like to live in Buenos Aires (where nearly half of the country's population resided) and so were seriously unprepared for ministering to inhabitants of a city. However, if the students were to share group-living in various areas of the metropolis, with professors teaching where students lived, their preparation would be very different. For the students, living in the safety and comfort of seminary buildings could imply being protected from encountering the way city people live. The administration and faculty found a new way to look at what they already knew.

What I have written in this book reflects the views of two significant educators, Sylvia Ashton Warner and Paulo Freire. Warner's work with children in New Zealand, described in her book *Teacher*, shows how important it is to begin where children are. She helped them learn to read and write by asking each child each day to give her a word to write on a card that would become, for the child, a "one look" word. These key, emotion-laden words not only led to writing, they keyed Warner into how the children lived and interpreted their worlds.

Paulo Freire became dangerous to Brazil because he helped peons connect their emotion-laden words, like boss, taxes, shovel, fence, horse or field, with written letters, that soon became stories the peons could write and read, thus helping them understand how the system in which they were caught kept them poor.

These experiences had informed my developing views about education which were eventually put together in *The Educating Act, A Phenomenological View*, issued by University Press of America, in 1981. Clearly those views inform the way I have attempted to gain a holistic understanding of the poverty system, and have led, obviously, to exploring what can be done to overcome this social blight. It makes vivid how responsibility depends on understanding, and that understanding depends on reflecting. Therefore this book seeks to engage you, and all of us, in looking at what you already know in order to discern our responsibilities in maintaining or overcoming that system. Failing to reflect does not relieve us from that responsibility, but when we act from habit or do the "usual," we may be responsible but are acting irresponsibly.

My unplanned educational experience has drawn me into a serious commitment. Writing about what I have learned has been prompted by accepting an invitation to give two lectures at the "First National Conference on Urban Issues," arranged by two former students, and sponsored by the State University of New York College at Buffalo; by conducting a nine-month Correspondence Seminar on Understanding Poverty in response to the Project's Board of Directors desire to become a study group; and by a member of that Board who said to me, "you have to write a book." So that is what I have done.

The hundreds of concerned and committed people with whom I have been engaged have been my teachers, showing me what goes on in their largely unappreciated programs, giving me new experiences, being for me a magnet of discovery and exploration. But some deserve special appreciation: my wife, Mildred, who introduced me to community activities in Greensboro where we had come to retire and where she soon became very active in the League of Women Voters; to those who have served on the Poverty Project's Board of Directors, particularly William C. Friday and the present Chair, Professor Charles E. Daye, for their patience, commitment, and wisdom; and for Mary F. Nies, who is a volunteer assistant with the Poverty Project and scrupulously examined every sentence in this book with professional care to be sure that it has been done correctly. I have been highly privileged.

———

The pylon pictured on the front is a "slatework" by the author.

Studies in the Postmodern Theory of Education

General Editors
Joe L. Kincheloe & Shirley R. Steinberg

Counterpoints publishes the most compelling and imaginative books being written in education today. Grounded on the theoretical advances in criticalism, feminism and postmodernism in the last two decades of the twentieth century, Counterpoints engages the meaning of these innovations in various forms of educational expression. Committed to the proposition that theoretical literature should be accessible to a variety of audiences, the series insists that its authors avoid esoteric and jargonistic languages that transform educational scholarship into an elite discourse for the initiated. Scholarly work matters only to the degree it affects consciousness and practice at multiple sites. Counterpoints' editorial policy is based on these principles and the ability of scholars to break new ground, to open new conversations, to go where educators have never gone before.

For additional information about this series or for the submission of manuscripts, please contact:

Joe L. Kincheloe & Shirley R. Steinberg
637 West Foster Avenue
State College, PA 16801